MW00785068

Lessons From the End of a Marriage

How I Found Happiness While Surviving Bigamy, Abandonment, and Deceit

Lisa Arends

Edited by Julie C. Hess

This is not based upon a true story; this IS a true story. However, some names and identifying details have been changed for the protection of the innocent and not-so-innocent.

Foreword

Perhaps you have found yourself at the end of a marriage and you are looking for meaning and purpose beyond the immediate pain and trauma. Maybe you are in a secure relationship and looking for lessons that will help to maintain the integrity of your union. Or, you may be single, looking for ways to understand yourself better and seeking happiness and balance in your life.

I think we all learn best through stories, narratives that frame the lessons of our lives. This book illustrates its lessons through the story of my divorce. It is an extreme example that involved years of deception, sudden abandonment, and felony bigamy. You may relate to some aspects of my story; I find that most people do. We all have been in positions where we have lost ourselves, all faced some sort of betrayal, and we all search for balance and happiness in our lives. Even if you have never been touched by this brand of pain (and I hope that you have not), you might find that you can learn from the lessons I found through my own trauma as I struggled to right myself after being knocked down.

Introduction

Sometimes, we have to have the floor ripped out from under us in order to realize that we are not balanced in our lives.

I used to think I was well. But, I wasn't. I thought I had balance. But, I didn't. I thought I was happy, but I didn't really know what happiness was. All it took to strip away all illusions of well-being were a few short sentences. It was a text from my husband, sent across the country on a sunny Saturday afternoon, that arrived unexpectedly on my phone.

July 11, 2009 12:38 p.m.

I'm sorry to be such a coward leaving you this way. I am leaving. Please reach out to someone let the dogs out as I am leaving the state. The code for the garage is 5914. I'm truly sorry but I can't do this anymore. Please give me some time to come to terms with my decision. I will call you in a few days. I am sorry that I have failed you.

Lesson One

When two becomes one, you are able to see yourself clearly.

Fear gripped. Legs collapsed. Brain stuttered. Lungs heaved. Gut clenched. Body trembled. World shattered. Visceral. Violent.

My father's arms engulfed me as I lay shaking on the floor. My body and brain rebelled from my new reality. I was buried by the pyroclastic flow of those words, pinned under the weight of the scalding lava sent through the phone lines. I looked like the fetal forms of the Pompeian's, caught unaware by the eruption of their worshipped Vesuvius.

"What can I do for you? Do you want me to call Mom?" my dad offered gently, seeking for a way to comfort his only child.

"Yes, please," I responded, forcing the words out through my locked lungs.

He reluctantly left me in a heap on the hallway floor in my aunt and uncle's house as he moved to the dining room to make the call to my mother in Texas, whom he had divorced decades earlier.

My brain barely registered his soft, yet strained voice in conversation several feet away from me. My hands gripped my phone with urgency, willing it to send another message. I wanted this to be a mistake. A joke. Anything but real. A little anger pushed through the initial shock, enough for me to summon the courage to flip open the

3

phone, using muscle memory trained over years to scroll down twelve names to Mr. T, the nickname he used, to put himself in the phone he bought for me years before.

"Hello. You've reached Timothy of MMS. I cannot come to the phone right now, but please leave a message and I will get back to you as soon as possible."

I took a deep breath and left a message, almost unintelligible through my tears, my shaking, and my heaving chest.

"Timothy. I don't understand. What is this? A text message? Sixteen years and a text message? Please don't do this. Not like this. Call me. Please."

I closed the phone, and severed the connection.

It sat there silent. Taunting me. I opened it again, but this time to send a text message.

What about the dogs? Are the dogs okay? Call me.

It remained silent. The screen remained dark.

My father was still in the other room, pacing the length of the dining room table as he and my mother searched for a plan. Meanwhile, my mind flashed upon the last week, looking for explanations. Answers. Anything.

Timothy had returned from a business trip on July 1, four days before I left our home in Atlanta to visit family on the West Coast. We had spent those few days together, enjoying each other's company as we took care of the mundane responsibilities of daily life and celebrated Independence Day. I searched the memories, looking for a clue, but none was forthcoming. He was as loving as always, never hinting that he was drafting the text while embracing me. On the morning of my trip, he walked with me into the airport, helping me with

4

check-in and baggage. Just outside security, next to the black and red poster declaring forbidden carry-on items, he hugged me fiercely. We kissed full passionate kisses. Pulling back slightly, he reassured me, "You'll be back before you know it. I love you and I'll see you soon." I just couldn't make sense of it all; how did this text come from the same man?

Nothing existed at those moments other than my broken body collapsed on the hardwood floor and my black and silver outdated Nokia flip phone. I alternated between gripping it until my fingertips were white from the pressure and flipping it open, willing a new message to appear on the screen. That phone, the deliverer of the death sentence of my marriage, was the only possible connection I had to my former life. It was my executioner and my security blanket in one.

My dad finally settled his body next to mine on the floor. He held my hand that was gripping the phone, his tenderness contrasting with my rigidity. He delivered the information from the call with a soothing voice, trying to keep himself calm and impart some comfort to me. My mom was going to call my friend Sarah to check on the dogs. My dad and I were going to immediately drive from Eugene, where we were visiting my aunt and uncle, back to Seattle, my dad's home in order to catch a plane back to Atlanta, where Timothy and I lived. My aunt came to us, crouching down so as not to loom over our crumpled bodies. After being informed of the plans, she lifted me onto the bed, where I was left with a box of tissues while my dad called his wife to have her arrange airline tickets.

The bed, although softer than the unyielding floor, offered no comfort. The tissues were simply something for my other hand to grip.

Shock had shut me down. As I lay curled on the bed, others packed my belongings and made the preparations to leave. I was helped off the bed and led out the door to my dad's waiting Miata, my things already placed in the trunk. I robotically pulled the seatbelt around my body, never lessening the grip on my phone in the process. The five hour drive was largely silent; I was still too stunned to speak and my dad's poor hearing didn't allow for conversation in the noisy car.

I used that time to reflect back on my marriage. Memories flashed through my mind like pages through a photo album.

Timothy and I met in 1993 at the Kerrville Folk Festival, a hippie-inspired haven outside of San Antonio. I had recently sworn off dating, but I welcomed a friendship with the funny, smart, and creative 16 year old. Although we were both from the San Antonio area, our homes were 30 minutes apart. Our early friendship was dependent upon the phone, as Timothy had no car and, as I was still 15, I had not yet obtained my license.

As weeks turned to months, our friendship became the primary force in both of our lives. He realized that our feelings had developed into love; I was too stubborn to see it yet, as I had decided to eliminate romance from my life.

The first time he told me he loved me, he said it in German. I did not translate it until he left that night.

Our first kiss was in my car, stopped outside his house, after our first time out alone together. It had been seven months since we met.

It was not a first kiss for either of us, but it felt so new and so powerful that I could feel my entire body swell with the emotion and passion of it. I realized I loved him. In English.

—
6

I decided to lift my ban on dating.

We had been inseparable in the 16 years since that kiss.

My memories were interrupted by the woodpecker sound of my phone ringing. My stomach dropped. I opened my hand, revealing the window on the cover of the phone, hoping, expecting, to see his name appear on the screen. Instead, my mom's name was emblazoned on the phone. I felt a strange blend of disappointment and relief, although I wanted, no *needed*, to talk to Timothy, although it was not a conversation to look forward to.

Opening the phone, I uttered, "Hey."

"Oh, sweetheart. I am so sorry," she said through sobs. "I talked to Sarah. She and Curtis went over to the house. The dogs are okay. It sounds like they were alone for a while, though. They were out of food and water and there was a mess all over the basement. She cleaned up and gave them food and water. They're okay now."

"Was there any sign of him? Anything?" I questioned.

"No. Curtis went with her, though, because they didn't know what they were walking in to. I warned her ahead of time that they may find him dead. He may be suicidal."

"I know. I thought that too", I replied. "None of this makes sense."

After hanging up with my mom, I called Sarah to thank her. I received one additional piece of information from her. She said there had been a letter placed on the kitchen island. She had not read it; its contents would remain unknown for another 12 hours until I could get back home.

The first leg of the journey came to an end as we pulled into my dad's driveway. The opening garage door revealed his wife, standing in the doorway, holding two plane tickets with my packed luggage and a bag for my dad by her side. After a brief stop to use the bathroom and say goodbye to his wife, we were back in the car, headed to the airport for our 9:20 p.m. departure to Atlanta.

We waited outside the last gate in the concourse to board our flight. The airport was slowing down for the night, the stores closing and more people were leaving than coming. I spent the time looking over the text messages from Timothy that I had received since he dropped me off at the airport six days earlier.

Mr T   7/5/09 6:49 am

> *Love ya!!! Have a smooth flight and be safe!*

Mr T   7/5/09 7:41 am

> *I told ya I'd stay in touch!*

Mr T   7/5/09 3:05 pm

> *Love you!!!*

Mr T   7/5/09 3:08 pm

> *Welcome to Seattle!*

Mr T   7/5/09 3:12 pm

> *Ok. For the record dill pickle cashews are really weird.*

Mr T   7/6/09 8:12 am

> *Morning to you too! Have a nice run?*

Mr T   7/6/09 8:14 am

> *Ha! I assumed you'd already be going out of your mind for a quick five miles. Did you have a good night last night?*

When he wrote the following three messages, he had already left the marital home and was on the road to his new life.

Mr T   7/10/09   11:14 am

> *We've had so much rain it sounds like a waterfall in the backyard!*

Mr T   7/11/09   12:10 pm

> *Hey! You okay?*

Mr T   7/11/09   12:12 pm

> *Sorry – I didn't know I'd missed your call until now. Love you big big!*

As I read these, I was compelled to send him another message.

7/11/09   5:54 p.m.

> *Sarah has dogs. My dad is taking me to Atlanta*
> *tonight. Where are you? Are you ok? I can't*
> *believe 16 years ending with a text.*

7/11/09   7:59 p.m.

> *Please just let me know if you're ok I'm worried*
> *about you*

My mom's texts to him, sent from her home in San Antonio, were even more concerned.

7/11/2009   3:39 PM

> *Is it true that you are leaving Lisa and the*
> *marriage? First, I need to verify that. If that is*
> *accurate, do you have specific plans as to*
> *when, etc. I am so very sorry this is happening,*
> *If it is. Cathy*

7/11/2009   7:32 PM

> *I'm worried about you. Are you OK? Core thing*
> *right now is to keep breathing. Medical stuff*
> *could be playing a big part in how you are*
> *feeling and thinking, distorting things a lot. Also,*
> *depression can have a genetic cause when*
> *there is family history of alcoholism. I care*
> *about you. How can I help? Please let me be of*

support. I love you and want you to be OK.
Remember, first thing is to keep breathing.

7/11/2009   7:37 PM

P.S. Depression and lack of sleep can both
really mess up thinking and feeling, getting
things really off base from what is really true.
I'm here for you if you want to talk or write.
Love, Mom

7/11/2009   7:48 PM

PPS-one other key factor to be aware of is the
effects and impact of burnout. I have been
concerned for years about your pace with work
and how that pace destroys a person over time.
When burnout accumulates, it can slide
downhill pretty quickly, being a huge wake call.

The flight was another endless yet timeless five hours. I was rigid in my seat against the window. My left hand gripped my dad's right and my own right hand still gripped the phone, even though it had been powered down for the flight.

Sunday, July 12, 2009

Early Sunday morning, I finally reached my house: relieved to finally be there, petrified of what I would find. The house felt empty, although I could hear the familiar sounds of the dogs barking from the basement. My eyes quickly scanned the rooms, searching for the "whys" and the "hows." I spotted a deliberately placed paper on the kitchen island and I began to read, scared to touch the paper, as though it would make the words somehow more real.

> *Lisa,*
>
> *I'm afraid there is no easy way for me to say this – I'm leaving. We have had a long and rich life together but I can no longer live this life anymore. As I told you several months ago, I feel as though we have been drifting apart for a number of years. It was a gradual thing but I can honestly say that it has reached a point where I no longer can share time with you without wondering when I can be away from you again. I can't keep living this lie – it's not fair to either one of us. I will continue to support you as best I can from wherever I end up. I will continue to work for DS but I would appreciate if you didn't involve them in this matter. We had some amazing times together and I will treasure these memories for the rest of my life. I think people change as they experience life and unfortunately we have grown so far apart that I simply cannot relate to you in any way. I know that this will hit you very hard*

and for that I am sincerely sorry. I have never wanted to do anything to harm you in any way but in doing so I have made myself unhappy for many years. I know that once you recover from the shock of this you will bounce back and live a happy and satisfying life – a better and more honest life than I could ever hope to offer you. Everything I have left behind is yours and all I have taken is my clothing and the equipment I need to make a living. I will never ask you for forgiveness or understanding. I am a coward who couldn't tell you to your face that I am leaving. If I don't do this now then I probably never will. I need my life to have some sort of meaning to it and unfortunately working in the basement of my house and watching tv and playing video games isn't it.

I'm sorry but my life is very quickly becoming that of my parents. No matter how much I see that, it feels like there is nothing I can do to change the path that I am on. From this point on there is nothing more that I can say other than how sorry I am for leaving you in this way. I will do everything I can fro this point forward to try and make this as easy on you as possible. I didn't strip the account to leave. I sold everything downstairs that I felt was part of the old me that I so desperately need to leave behind.

Sixteen years.

Sixteen *wonderful* years.

Half my life.

A text message.

A *fucking* text message.

A letter left behind.

A typed, unsigned letter.

How could something so rich, so all-encompassing, end so succinctly and so impersonally? Summed up and dismissed in 140 words or less.

My fear became frustration at his lack of response. I sent him one last message via e-mail, imploring him to step up and deal with the business of the break up. I expected no response and my expectations were fulfilled.

> *7/12/09   7:47 a.m.*
>
> *I've been mentally composing this for hours to try to not make it sound too angry. Coming home to a "dear John" letter and finding that you had cleared out while I was away fueled my fire again. I just keep thinking that your last employer got a sit down meeting when you quit while I got a text. You have been telling me, through words and actions, that it was okay & then this? You say you want to be supportive, but I can't see that right now. I can't think of a more painful way to do this. I can't believe you stranded me across the country with this news, with no money, and the responsibility of the dogs. I may well bounce back, but this has*

14

shattered me to the core. I gave you time & opportunity before - why do it like this? I would like to think that your love & respect for me would override your cowardice. Please show me that respect now by talking to me - it is time to stop hiding.

You will need to come back soon from wherever you are so that we can disentangle our lives. As much as you may want to shirk responsibilities, we have a house, etc. that we need to make decisions about and I guess we need to file paperwork. I don't know my plans yet, but can't stay in the home we built together.

Needing action, but having no direction, I purged the closet of his leftover clothes and shoved them into garbage bags intended for Goodwill. I grabbed his books, stacking them in the garage. It felt purposeful. As I moved throughout the house, I found some details that caused me pause: a wine glass in the dishwasher, a new scent on the sheets, a guest towel in the hamper. These finds caught my attention, yet were minor enough to occupy only the recesses of my mind.

My dad went to work in Timothy's office, clearing the custom basement room of the detritus of Timothy's life while he searched for clues that would provide some answers. No answers were unearthed; only more questions arose. Why did he take all of the financial records after 2005? Why was there a prescription for Cialis? Did he take his computers and software, or sell them as implied in the letter? And most importantly, *why* did he do this?

The normalcy evident in certain areas of the house haunted me. He had done my laundry and placed my folded clothes in their normal location. The fridge had been cleaned out of perishable foods. The cat's litter had been changed and the dishwasher run. As he was packing his car to leave his life behind, he continued to live its details.

The house that night was vacuous. Alien. Familiar.

Haunted.

Artifacts of a shared life strewn about that taunted me. Whispering false hopes.

Since he would not respond to me, I began to find myself having imaginary conversations with him, responding to his letter. My first interpretation was one of shock, anger, and disbelief.

"Dear John" letter – First Interpretation (July 12, 2009)

Lisa, I'm afraid there is no easy way for me to say this – I'm leaving. *Yeah – I got that from the text message. Thanks.* We have had a long and rich life together but I can no longer live this life anymore. *Why is this in the past tense; you sent me loving messages mere hours ago?* As I told you several months ago, I feel as though we have been drifting apart for a number of years. *And I was furious that you kept that hidden for a number of years and only told me when I pulled it out of you.* It was a gradual thing but I can honestly say that it has reached a point where I no longer can share time with you without wondering when I can be away from you again. *Knife through the gut, twisted. Why do you always tell me you miss me and can't wait to see me again?* I can't keep living this lie – it's not fair to either one of us. *True – this is not fair to me.* I will continue to support you as best I can from wherever I end up. *That's nice, but not my first concern. Where are you? Are you drifting on the currents?* I will continue to work for DS but I would appreciate if you didn't involve them in this matter. *Strange. Why are you mentioning your employer?* We had some amazing times together and I will treasure these memories for the rest of my life. *I agree that it has been amazing; I am not sure how much I'll be able to treasure them after this ending. Besides, if you have been unhappy for years, when*

17

were the times real? When did you begin to pretend? I think people change as they experience life and unfortunately we have grown so far apart that I simply cannot relate to you in any way. *You were relating just fine yesterday – what the hell happened?* I know that this will hit you very hard and for that I am sincerely sorry. *Apology not accepted.* I have never wanted to do anything to harm you in any way but in doing so I have made myself unhappy for many years. *WHY DIDN'T YOU TALK TO ME?* I know that once you recover from the shock of this you will bounce back and live a happy and satisfying life – a better and more honest life than I could ever hope to offer you. *This sounds rather blithe; do you actually think that I can recover from this like it is a case of the flu? Honest is a strange word choice.* Everything I have left behind is yours and all I have taken is my clothing and the equipment I need to make a living. *I'm not exactly worried about stuff at this point. I did notice, however, that you took all of the financial records along with the computer that is used to pay bills. Interesting.*

I will never ask you for forgiveness or understanding. *Good. Because they are in rather short supply right now.* I am a coward who couldn't tell you to your face that I am leaving. *Coward is exactly right.* If I don't do this now then I probably never will. *Why now?* I need my life to have some sort of meaning to it and unfortunately working in the basement of my house and watching tv and playing video games isn't it. *Your choice to do those things.*

I also noticed that you took most of the DVDs and video games. Interesting. I'm sorry but my life is very quickly becoming that of my parents. *How? You are so different from your father; we are so different than their marriage.* No matter how much I see that, it feels like there is nothing I can do to change the path that I am on. *That doesn't sound like drifting. Where does this path go?* From this point on there is nothing more that I can say other than how sorry I am for leaving you in this way. *You should be.* I will do everything I can from this point forward to try and make this as easy on you as possible. *So we start off as difficult as possible and then you want to be helpful? I wonder what "easy as possible" will look like?* I didn't strip the account to leave. *Why is this here? Does this relate to the strange bills I received while you were in Brazil last month?* I sold everything downstairs that I felt was part of the old me that I so desperately need to leave behind. *Did you sell the computers? Games? Software? Most of what I see missing is what you need to make a living. Did you sell your work equipment? Something here doesn't feel right.*

My biggest fear had always been losing him; I could not imagine a future without him by my side.

I had never been an adult without Timothy.

I now faced a life without a life-mate.

He had become fully enmeshed in my existence. Teasing the strings of him out of me would take time and a patient hand. I needed to find where he ends and I begin.

After being together for so long and from such an early age, I really didn't know who I was without him. Of course, we had our own interests, our own friends and hobbies, but no area was untouched by the other in some way. I defined myself through him. I was part of a partnership.

Weeks earlier, in a summer staff development session at school, I was asked to write three words that defined me. After a moment's consideration, I wrote:

Wife

Runner

Teacher

Now, all of those were in doubt. Who was I now? By fracturing the bond that had joined two into one, he had forced me to begin to define myself. By myself. The first step in reclaiming my life and finding balance would be to see myself clearly.

Lesson Two

When you lose everything, you take nothing for granted.

From those first tentative moments as teenagers in the Texas Hill Country to that final embrace at the Atlanta airport, Timothy and I had a great relationship according to any ordinary metrics. We dated throughout our junior and senior years of high school and never suffered from the drama that plagues so many young relationships. We bonded over backgrounds and grew together through tragedy with our connection becoming stronger with every passing day.

He came from a rough home. An only child who's parents were both alcoholics. His mom was a very fearful and lonely woman who would turn to him for support as her blood alcohol levels rose. He grew accustomed to spending his evenings comforting her while trying to dodge his father. His dad grew belligerent when he drank, instigating arguments and fights until he passed out on the couch; the dogs curled by his feet.

He turned to the Boy Scouts in elementary school for parental guidance and a sense of family. By the time I met him, he had assumed a leadership position in scouting and spent his summers working as a counselor at a nearby camp. He took his position seriously; he would spend hours preparing lessons and awards for the young scouts. The other counselors became his brothers and the troop leaders, his parents. He told me on more than one occasion that the Boy Scouts had saved his life.

When we first met, I was immediately drawn to him. He had that gangly giraffe body that most teenage boys seem to assume for a time, but he had the most amazing intelligent and mischievous green eyes peering out from beneath his long brown hair. He was silly and sarcastic. Smart and articulate. Even then, I was a sucker for a good lesson and I could tell that he had much that he could teach me.

Much of our early relationship followed the usual patterns of young love: we spent hours on the phone, wrote countless notes to each other when we should have been transcribing lectures, and looked forward to weekends out. His friends became mine and mine grew into his. Our kisses progressed and we explored our burgeoning sexuality together.

In many ways, our courtship was customary. But it was also marred by multiple tragedies, which shaped each of us as individuals and also sculpted our relationship. In the three-year span which marked the end of our teenage years, we each suffered the unexpected loss of several friends and mentors. The reasons were diverse: accidents, suicides, murder. But the results were the same. We were continually bowled over by shock and grief. We each were looking for answers and searching for assurance.

For my part, I tried to weather each storm as it came. I had an advantage in this realm as I was raised by a counselor. All those, "Let's talk about its" and "How do you feel about thats" had taught me some skills I could apply as I navigated the grief. Even then, by the time I was 18 and attending college in Austin, I needed help in the form of therapy and medication.

Timothy didn't have it so easy. He had one loss that weighed especially heavily: his scoutmaster committed suicide during Timothy's senior year. This man was a mentor and father figure. Timothy looked up to him and emulated him. The death was complicated by the fact that it was surrounded by rumors of the perpetration of sexual abuse and Timothy's name was mentioned specifically in the suicide note. I never knew in what context. Timothy lost his innocence the day he received the call that delivered the news of the suicide. He lost a part of himself that day that I don't think he ever got back.

At the time, his pain was buried beneath our growing enthusiasm for the end of high school and the beginning of our lives together. I believed his assurances he was okay and was more than ready to leave childhood behind and begin my adulthood with him.

I moved from San Antonio to Austin in the summer of 1995 for college. I specifically chose a living arrangement that would allow Timothy to spend the night, as he was still living and working as a road hand in San Antonio. The first several weeks were fine, but in October, as word of two more deaths reached me, I quickly spiraled into a deep depression.

Timothy was my first responder.

He knew immediately that I could not be there. He packed up my things and drove me to his parents' house in San Antonio. He was my compass and my cane as I received the medical and psychiatric care I needed. Within months, I was off antidepressants and functioning normally, although I would not return to Austin again.

He had seen me at my most vulnerable, my most fragile, and he carried me through to the other side of my anguish and despair. I loved him more than ever.

I had already learned so much from him.

I learned the value in being willing to embrace the humor in a moment without concern for other's opinions when he dressed as a clown for my eighteenth birthday. I learned how to accept touch and another's proximity as he sat behind me each day after high school as I ate my dinner. I learned the value of honor as he slept on the floor next to my bed while holding my hand through the night so that we would not break the house rules set forth by his mom. I learned the extent of love when he gave a tender kiss on my bloodied mouth after a complicated wisdom tooth removal operation. I learned the possibilities of passion in the backseat of a '56 Chevy that got stuck in the mud by a river. I even tried to learn to play chess, but that one didn't stick.

I was excited about entering life with him and looking forward to new lessons.

We rented our first apartment together just after my nineteen birthday. Within a month, we purchased a pug we christened Mad Max, who filled our little place with lots of kisses and wiggles. And poop. Who can forget the poop? That adorable wrinkled devil had an uncanny ability to climb over the baby gate designed to secure her in the bathroom, tear into her bag of dog food, and after consuming copious quantities of kibble, leave the remnants all over the apartment. Even as we cursed her bowels, we loved that little dog and all that she symbolized for us.

Max brought a wonderfully roguish spirit into our home. She was brilliant and feisty and brought us no end of entertainment. One afternoon, after coming home from work, Timothy went to take a shower. He scoffed at the claim that I could teach Max how to "crawl" by the time he was out. She had mastered the trick before he even had a chance to wash his hair.

As our first "child," Max was properly spoiled. She went everywhere with us, earning the nickname "All-Terrain Pug" for her ability to handle hikes that were treacherous for creatures ten times her size. All three of us had an "us against the world" attitude and we bonded against some imagined front.

We did not have much money in those early days. I had returned to school in San Antonio, and I had short-term jobs at a pet store, a gym, and a tanning salon. Timothy had left the uncertainty of the stagehand union, with the exception of a single movie in Houston, to take a job as a carpenter for Sea World. We paid bills together and laid out our financial goals and plans as a team. This period was a time for trust-building, and he always came through with flying colors.

After meeting as teenagers, we entered adulthood together as partners, best friends, confidents, and lovers.

After his stint at Sea World led to another financial dead end, we realized that we would have to leave San Antonio behind in order to secure a living. Leaving Texas meant that I was abandoning the majority of my studies thus far and my plan of entering into a career of physical therapy, but I did not mind. It was more important for me to be near him.

He was the first to leave. He packed his car and drove the 900 miles to Atlanta with his father, where they had both secured

25

employment. For seven months, I had my first taste of life without him while I remained in San Antonio to finish out the semester. The apartment felt hollow and the pug and new kitten did little to fill the empty space. I filled my days with work, school, friends and family. But still I felt a void. A gap like that left by a pulled tooth where he had been. Making the wait even more unbearable was the fact that we were to be married that upcoming winter.

Around this time, I took over primary responsibility for the finances since I had more time available. We already had joint accounts that we built up together. We made smart financial decisions and were clear on the fact that we wanted to have financial security. We were careful with money and avoided debt and lived within our slowly expanding means.

The days passed. Hours on the phone rekindled memories of our childhood romance. His twenty-second birthday came and went. A dress bought. A wedding planned. Finals taken and boxes packed. And, finally, after many sleepless nights, we were reunited.

We were married on the beach in Florida on a warm December day. It was a planned elopement of sorts; we decided we did not want any family present. The wedding was officiated by a gay Methodist pastor who looked like David Lee Roth and threatened to marry us while wearing his yellow Speedo. Luckily, it was only a threat. The witness was a newspaper photographer that we hired to do our wedding photos because we both hated posed shots. She followed us as we walked for miles along the empty beach after we exchanged our vows, capturing our spontaneous embraces and our glowing smiles.

26

It was a beautiful day. We had arrived at the hotel the afternoon before, after driving down from Atlanta. We immediately "christened" the room and then had a wonderful evening having dinner at the hotel restaurant, exploring the beach, and playing in the outdoor pool. We slept in the morning of our wedding, awaking to sun streaming in through the curtained windows. After a brief jaunt to have my hair fashioned in a causal up-do, we went back to the room to finish getting ready. When the pastor knocked on our door, we calmly sat on the sofa, legs intertwined, each with a book in hand. He commented that we were the most relaxed couple he had ever seen prior to exchanging vows. We were relaxed because we had no doubts. No hesitations. We had been married in our hearts years before and the addition of the rings did not change a thing.

The early years of our marriage were characterized by us making our marks on the world: finding our place and creating our space. Timothy hopscotched through the trade show and movie industries, moving from the shop floor to creating designs from behind a computer. I switched my major to education once we moved to Atlanta. I immediately secured a job as a middle school math teacher upon graduation and found success in the classroom. We purchased a house months after the wedding: a home with more promise than pizazz that we immediately began to personalize. We worked late into the night with Pink Floyd on the stereo and a snoring pug curled up by the warmth of the compound miter saw. Our elderly neighbors would frequently peek into our front window in the evening, curious about the young couple emulating Bob Vila.

We settled into married life. We collected two more dogs and many more friends. The one thing noticeably absent from our marriage was a child. That was intentional. We knew from a very young age that we wanted to remain childless. We each had our reasons: he was concerned about the genetics in his family and didn't want to risk passing them on and I never had a draw to young children and had no desire to be a mother. We made the decision permanent mere weeks after the wedding when he had a vasectomy. It was an unusual step for a 22 year old couple, but we were sure and never regretted our choice.

If there was a breach in the hull of our marriage, it would have been in our work habits. We were both very driven people; we took pride in our jobs and never hesitated to work longer and harder to make things just a little bit better. He worked long hours on the road and longer hours on the computer, often designing late into the night. I spent weekends writing curriculum and weeknights tutoring students. We both had a tendency to find our self-worth through our jobs and to seek validation through our paychecks. This left him in a vulnerable place when he faced some professional setbacks later in the marriage.

Around 2005, when I returned to school to get my master's, he took over as the Minister of Finance, since he had greater access to the computer and phone than I did. We talked about finances frequently and had a policy of discussing any single purchase over $100 with the other person. I didn't look at many accounts, but I was occasionally shown PDF documents that corresponded to accounts. PDF documents that I now know were faked. At the time, I never dreamed that he would use his graphic design skills and software to deceive me.

Our marriage was untainted by the hardships that face many. We were always best friends; we communicated easily and often. We worked together as a team and tackled tasks equally and shared responsibilities. We enjoyed a healthy sexual relationship that never faded even in the final days of the marriage. I had his back, and I always felt like he had mine. We had a true partnership. Little did I know my wedding ring was fabricated from fool's gold.

Monday, July 13, 2009

It is so easy to become complacent with what you have. To not appreciate those things which one views as constant. To not be aware of what is, until it is not. Until something is lost, its full value is not known.

I began to realize just how much I had lost early that Monday morning as the clicks of the zipper on the body bag of my life became too loud to ignore.

Sunday night. Infinite.

I arose from my vigil on the sofa at 3:00 a.m. and was immediately drawn to the computer. The wireless was weak in my office (the signal booster was apparently in the category of "the equipment I need to make a living"), so I relocated to the kitchen island. I desperately checked e-mail. No message from him. Pressing refresh repeatedly did not change anything. It didn't stop me from trying.

I needed information. Facts amongst the uncertainty he left behind. I started with the company that held our checking and savings accounts, insurance, and mortgage. I knew his member number, and had known the user name and password previously.

"Incorrect user name and/or password."

"Access denied."

He changed them.

Luckily, one of the benefits of being together so long, I knew the answers to his verification questions.

"What was your high school mascot?"

Rockets

"What city did you go to elementary school in?"

Kirby

"What is your mother's maiden name?"

You're kidding me. That's all you've got?

Logged in, I first noticed a credit card listed at the top of the page (balance $51,070.42) that I was not aware existed.

Fear. Dread. Panic. Anger. What the fuck was going on?

The unknown credit card was only the beginning. The balance in the checking account, bold in scarlet type, was -$197.66. Yeah. Negative. I sat on the high stool, my forearms pressed hard into the granite of the kitchen island. My head shook side to side as I tried to comprehend the text on the screen in front of me and my legs picked up the pace of tremors so that the chair made clicking noises against the tile floor. The dogs, sensing my growing panic, entered into their own choreography around my feet.

I clicked on the checking account to bring up the activity sheet, looking for the reasons behind the unexpected number. As soon as I glanced at the entries, I knew that I couldn't do this alone. I pulled myself up the stairs, legs trembling so hard that I could feel the tendons pull taught against the bones. I crawled into bed next to my dad who had passed out in the guest room after midnight. My shaking moved the entire bed. The dogs' nails clicked on the wood floor as they entered the room behind me.

My voice soft, yet strained, I managed to communicate my needs. "I need you. Finances. He maxed out a credit card that I didn't know existed. He spent thousands in Brazil. And there's evidence of an affair." He followed me to the kitchen island, which was soon to be information central. A command center set up in a disaster zone.

I scrolled down the list of charges, categorizing, explaining, interpreting. Looking for understanding.

He had been in Brazil for the last two weeks in June on what I was told was a business trip. The checking account told another story. The money hemorrhaged from the account over the duration of the trip. Thousands spent at hotels and bars. Restaurants and shops. ATM withdrawals several times a day. Overdraft fees were peppered through the reports and punctuated the rollercoaster ride of the balance as money was moved around. There were bills that spoke of high alcohol consumption and numbers that indicated a partner in crime.

In the months leading up to Brazil, he frequently enjoyed (at least I am assuming he had a good time) lunches at pubs while running up $70 tabs according to the charges I saw on the accounts. On the evenings I tutored, he must have snuck out of the neighborhood behind me because the account indicated he would be at a bar down the street rather than down in his office as purported.

I could not go on. I could not stop. The more I saw, the more I knew. The more I read, the less I understood. I did not want to see, but I had to look at the wreckage of my marriage spelled out in an account statement. The demise of my union itemized and categorized in neat little rows. As if taunting me, the normal expenses of daily life were embedded within the horrors: a grocery trip, topping off the tank, a trip to Home Depot to buy more caulk. The two lives he lived stood in relief on the accounts.

I looked back further and sought more answers. Looking for the moment when the man I loved stole my heart along with my paycheck. I realized that the affair, at least the current one, began in March. Shortly after that, there was evidence of repeated trips to Iowa, conveniently covered up with tales of visiting his company's headquarters in Michigan. The spending was reckless, showing no constraint, as he spent a premium on last-minute flights and rental cars. That was just a hint of the financial discoveries to come.

My dad and I sat at the kitchen island scrolling through months and years of activity on multiple accounts. Every page, every PDF, every website brought news of more deception. It was clear that financial collapse was inevitable. The C-4 had been set. The detonator triggered. He jumped out the window to escape the explosion and left me behind, stunned and blind, in the conflagration of our lives.

We could see a pattern emerging from the documents. The irresponsible spending started out (apparently in 2005) generally slow and controlled (if there can be such a thing), and only touched accounts in his name. As time progressed, his restraint lifted and he showed no boundaries to his spending. One particular account illustrated the complexity of his lies. In 2007, he and I spent several weeks discussing refinancing the house and rolling the remaining balance on an old $10,000 home equity line into the note. We looked at the website. I was next to him while he was on the phone with the company. The next week, he pulled me out of my classroom at work to sign the papers, knowing my single-mindedness while I was at the school.

There was no refinance.

It was a home equity line for $50,000. He bled the account in less than four months. The activity was frenetic, scattered. Money shifted constantly between accounts to ensure that the anticipated balances were always present. His office had turned into an airport control tower which carefully guided payments, debits, and transfers in order to avoid a catastrophic collision. I could not tell where the money was going or where it went. Other than the last few months with the affair, the money simply disappeared, much of it in the form of cash withdrawals or payments made to new and unknown credit cards whose activity statements I could not access. He had executed a perfect David Copperfield act: distract me while making the money disappear. Except I wasn't applauding the performance.

My dad, a pacifist in the truest sense, became angry as the reality of Timothy's malicious irresponsibility set in.

"No matter what else I did, I always made sure that you were taken care of financially. It almost pushed me into bankruptcy myself," he softly stated while scrolling through one of the accounts, tears brimming in his eyes.

"I know," I responded with a hug.

Like my dad, I am an action person. We decided to contact the companies, starting with the one that held the majority of the accounts. We were out of our element, both being responsible bill-paying citizens. I was too scared and my body was shaking too hard to make the calls myself.

My dad cried every time he explained the situation to the person on the phone. I had only seen my dad cry once before this experience. Now he was tearing up all the time. The shock had shattered his defenses as much as mine. We were raw.

The hours were filled with overwhelming hopelessness.

We took a break to go to the credit union, where I opened up a new dis-joint account and arranged for my direct deposit to be moved. The account was seeded with money generously donated from my uncle David and my mom and I was due to receive my bimonthly paycheck in a few days. Accomplishment.

Back at the house, we switched our focus to trying to locate a divorce attorney. My plan was to cut all ties as quickly as possible and build a firewall between him and me so that I could look forward, my own Great Wall, only my husband was the marauding horde I needed protection from.

In a brief phone consultation with one lawyer, the word, "bankruptcy" was brought up for the first time.

Bankruptcy.

Devastating. Shameful.

Protection.

Hope?

I felt a little better as some items were ticked off the list. Forty-eight hours out, and I was resolved to the fact that he was gone. I just wanted to move forward. Get through. Get out. Get on.

By this time, the framework of support had been decided: my dad took the first shift by default; my mom would follow up and stay with me until the start of the school year, just two weeks away.

I felt like I needed to clean up some of his loose ends. I found his baby book when I was shifting through the remnants of our lives. I contemplated contacting his parents, who lived just two streets over, but decided against it, as I was unsure of their role in all of this. Instead, we drove by his parent's house and I tucked the baby book in the bushes around the mailbox.

I called his boss.

"I just thought that you should know that Timothy sent me a text on Saturday while I was in Seattle that said he was leaving. He is not here and his computers are gone."

"I don't get involved in personal…"

"I just want you to know. From what I understand, some of the computers are property of the company and he is still employed with you."

"Yes."

"They are gone and I do not know where they are and I do not know where he is. Bye."

My impression was that his boss knew about the affair. I wondered how he would feel if he was the victim of the deceit? The one whose life had been thrown out like a pair of old socks?

As I hung up the phone, I looked at the dogs, still gathered around the base of the kitchen island. The tension obvious in their postures. I turned to my dad, tears already pouring from my swollen eyes.

"I can't keep them."

I was forced into one of the most difficult and painful decisions of my life. Even before the revelation of the financial disaster, I knew that I would not be able to stay in the home or, more tragically, care for our three dogs. I took the responsibility of them very seriously; we chose to adopt them and their well-being was entirely in our hands. Timothy robbed me of my ability to care for them financially, physically, or emotionally. It was not fair to them to keep them in my care. They were already suffering from the tension in the home and the lack of attention. The best thing I could do for them was to place them in good homes. We had just over two weeks to try to place two elderly and one middle age dog in loving homes. It would not be easy.

I could not face the job of securing homes for the dogs. Perhaps it was cowardly, but I knew that I did not have the strength to promise them to another.

"If Mom helps me give the dogs up, can you help me find homes? I don't think I can do it." I asked my dad and sobs broke through the words.

"I sure will," he responded, voice cracking.

We both began to weep, holding each other to try to dull the pain. The dogs watched.

I began to talk through my thoughts about the future. I knew I needed to get away, to escape from the kudzu curtain that swathed me in suffocating memories. His running away had necessitated mine, as my home had become a prison. My first instinct was to leave Atlanta completely behind. I only moved here for his job, and I had no family in town. I considered an immediate exit to Seattle or San Antonio where my respective parents lived. Even though my fractured heart wanted away from any and all reminders, my brain luckily still had a little kick to it.

I had a teaching job secured for the following year at a school where I had worked for eight years and which was filled with friends and a support system. I knew I had a legal mountain ahead of me and that monolith would be easier to climb if I stayed in the area. I realized that I needed to remain in Atlanta until the end of the school year. And then I would be free.

Adrenaline kept me going. By Monday night, I had been over three days without sleep and more than two without food. As I don't operate with much in reserve in either area, my body was shutting down. The health I had always taken for granted was dissipating along with the tears. As I was trying to excise him from my mind, my body was violently trying to rid itself of anything held inside, as though the text was delivered with a bolus of syrup of ipecac. Even my period, which had been coming to an end that weekend, picked up with a vengeance. I bled for over two weeks. Perhaps it was my body's way of weeping.

Sleep was still elusive that night, but I lacked the energy to leave the couch. I was a husk, sloughing off memories, as I lay as an interloper in the living room of my marriage.

Tuesday, July 14, 2009

I began to stir as the first light began to pierce through the curtains. I moved through the familiar dance of feeding and letting the

---

37

dogs out, painfully aware that the curtain call on that particular performance would be quickly upon me. I sobbed from the deck as I watched the dogs make their morning rounds. I had been holding it in until they moved away from my side; I didn't want to upset them any further.

My dad and I were both in a daze that morning, moving about but accomplishing nothing. I realized that I could not stay in the house any longer. I had not slept in four days and rest was impossible within its traitorous walls. Sarah, the savior of the dogs while I was traveling, offered me a room in her home.

"Stay with me," she said, veracity and stubbornness shining behind her pale blue eyes.

I was stunned at the offer. "It would probably be for the school year," I tentatively replied.

"No problem; I'll get the room ready."

"Thank you, thank you so much," I said, the tears beginning again. I glanced at the animals sleeping in the sun shining through the French doors. The cat had joined her canine siblings.

"You can bring her," Sarah said, nodding towards the cat. "Curtis would love it."

"Thank you," I replied, "I think I'll try to keep her."

Feeling bolstered by the accomplishment of finding a shelter for me, we turned our attention to finding homes for the dogs. I knew I could not care for them, but I also could not leave them at the regular animal shelter. Two of the dogs were older, and faced almost certain death in that competitive environment.

My dad had already helped to secure the two lawyers: divorce and bankruptcy. His next agenda was to locate homes for the dogs. It was not an easy task for a lifelong dog lover who frequently fosters animals. His wife started by contacting Seattle shelters and navigating through the network while he began an e-mail blitz from Atlanta.

Pet lovers-

Due to a family crisis, we have three wonderful dogs that need a new home. My daughter is being forced out of her home due to abrupt spousal abandonment (after 16 years) and his blatant and deceitful financial irresponsibility.

As she soon will be living in a rented room, she will not be able to keep her three beloved dogs. The three have been together since puppies and can easily live together. We have already called friends and neighbors to see if they could take one or all of them, with no success. There is also a cat, however we have found her a home. The dogs and cat also got along well.

The particulars:

Max: 13 year old female Pug (Southeast Pug rescue has been contacted too). We know she is probably not adoptable, but we want her to be comfortable in her final time.

Porter: Nine year old male Boston Terrier about 25 pounds.

Glottis: Six year old female Lab/Border Collie mix about 45 pounds.

Ideally Porter and Glottis would stay together and Max could go to a Pug rescue agency.

All three are in good health for their respective ages and are neutered.

We are in the Lawrenceville area and have transportation available in the Atlanta area.

This situation has arisen very quickly (in the last three days) and become urgent. We will need to do something early next week.

I'm sending this (her father) since she is not able to function well at this time.

Tommy Arends

Thank you very much for any assistance or recommendations you can provide.

All of the no-kill shelters were full.

I packed a small bag for the night. My dad drove me to the grocery store and then to Sarah's. It felt like some horrific perversion of a childhood sleepover, but I was so grateful to have a blank slate for the night. I ate my first meal: half of a gluten free Redbridge beer and a piece of Ian's gluten free French toast, while I was sitting on the floor as my dad and Sarah talked.

My dad ate, too, soup and crackers while sitting at the coffee table. He looked more relaxed than I had seen him. As he stood to leave, he thanked Sarah for taking me in and tears yet again pored down his normally dry face.

I had my first two hours of sleep that night.

Wednesday, July 15, 2009

On Wednesday, my dad and I first met with the divorce attorney. She immediately set me at ease, as she exuded a comforting combination of confidence and empathy. We laid out the sordid story and showed her the "Dear John" letter.

"So I assume you want to try for mediation," she responded.

I liked this lady.

We emphasized that I wanted to sever ties as quickly as possible so that I could begin to move forward. We learned that the divorce would most likely have to be done by publication since Timothy's whereabouts were unknown and he had not responded to any attempts to contact him. This meant that the divorce notice would run in the county newspaper for 60 days before the divorce could be finalized. It felt absurd; I may have as well filed for divorce via carrier pigeon with the impersonal nature of the newspaper. I was so glad that he had decided to make this as "easy on me as possible" (insert sarcasm here).

I filled out the necessary paperwork and signed the first of many large checks to initiate the legal separation from him. Within a few short days, divorce had gone from the last thing I ever wanted to the thing I wanted the most.

That afternoon, we moved my clothing and work materials over to my new sanctuary.

I had an upstairs bedroom and bathroom, with a corner of a bonus room for an office. I had gone from 2,500 square feet to 250. It was perfect.

41

Their home was comfortable and supportive, and filled with the sounds of a young baby.

It was alive.

Within its walls, I could begin to envision a life independent of Timothy. I was away from the immediate reminders, and was free to dream of the future.

I felt compelled to write, something I had never done outside the requirements of a classroom. Before returning to my old house to care for the dogs, my dad agreed to take me to buy the necessary tools to begin a journal. I stood in the school supply aisle at Target for several minutes until I finally selected a three-subject spiral notebook adorned with a lively green patterned cover. I decided that I would commit to writing in three parts that corresponded to the sections within the notebook: spewing the poison, mulling the present, and dreaming about the future. I would start with the first, bleeding off some of the anger and energy, and finish with the last with the intention that it would leave me with hope and positive feelings.

My first entry reveals the shock, my thoughts as muddled as a three-year-old's finger-painting.

"A blank page – my life on 7/11. How could you be so cruel, so cold, so two-faced? How long? Why? Were you deceiving yourself as much as me?"

"Sarah – what a true friend. She reminds me that I am not alone and that life goes on."

"In a strange way, I have never been so free. Options are open. For the first time, I will be able to choose where I live and how I live."

With those words, I closed the journal and sobbed quietly through the night.

Thursday, July 16, 2009

The accounts had whispered some of the story to me: Timothy had gotten into trouble with money, he had an affair, and he was currently in Iowa with another person. That sketchy framework still did not explain where the money went or what had precipitated all of this. I needed more information.

Our e-mail addresses were both through the same domain that we had purchased when he started his own company a few years earlier. My dad and I soon discovered, that with a few menu option changes, we could see his junk mail file. I became addicted, hitting "get mail" like a gambling junkie on a slot machine.

At that point, all of the mail was innocuous, advertising interspersed with copious quantities of iTunes receipts. At least I could rest easy, knowing that he had good music wherever he was.

That e-mail inbox, although designed for junk, was soon to become anything but, as it revealed truths that would have serious consequences.

Friday, July 17, 2009

As that first week progressed, more overdue accounts surfaced. A knock on the door brought a Rooms To Go notice threatening charge-off for an account in my name. Letters demanding payment came for several cards in his name, some of which I never knew existed. Getting the mail each day was a two-hour affair: I spent an hour gearing myself for the walk down the driveway and an hour recovering from what I found. I knew that I could not continue to live this way.

My dad's shift in Atlanta was drawing to a close; my mom was to take over the next day. My dad and I had one last task on our list: the bankruptcy attorney.

This task left me overwhelmed with shame and fear. I had always been conservative with money. Too conservative. I was the kid who took a school trip to Europe and only spent money on food and bathrooms, returning my traveler's checks to my mom upon my arrival back home. As an adult, I worked hard to build up my financial well-being, a job I thought Timothy shared with me. In the last few years, I had obtained my master's degree to secure a pay raise and I worked several hours a week as a math tutor to bring in additional funds.

And now it was gone. And, because of the nature of a marriage, it was unclear to the outside world who was the emptier of the accounts. He had concocted some great Ponzi scheme and then disappeared, leaving me to face those he swindled.

Friday morning brought the meeting with the bankruptcy attorney. My right leg, whose violent shaking had calmed somewhat since the meeting with the divorce lawyer, picked up its incessant rhythm once again. I was petrified of receiving news about additional unknown accounts. The paralegal had run my credit report. The last time I had seen it, about two years earlier, it was pristine, spotless. I could not face it now. My dad offered to check the report, scanning it for evidence of accounts that we had not yet discovered. There were none.

Inhale.

We were told that the accounts in his name would not matter in the case of personal bankruptcy.

Exhale.

It sounded as though my name would be removed from the note on the house and the home equity line.

Inhale.

I could protect myself from his debts and be able to rebuild.

Exhale.

The staccato trembling of my leg began to ease again.

As we sat around a large, cherry-stained conference table meeting with the bankruptcy attorney and her paralegal, my husband was making a vow that would change our lives forever.

That task done and one more check written, we now faced a lull in the action. We were spent both figuratively and literally. It was time to switch gears.

We pulled up at the movie theater.

"Two for Borat, please," my dad said to the teen in the window as he handed over his card.

"Sir, I have to inform you that the movie is especially graphic and may be offensive to some viewers. There are no refunds," the ticket-taker recited automatically.

My dad and I looked at each other, the first true laughs of the week expelled in staccato bursts.

"Welcome to the South," I said to him with a grin. Besides, nothing on that movie screen could be more offensive than my reality.

Undeterred by the warning, we proceeded to the theater where we shared more laughs and a much needed respite from the reality outside those doors.

In under a week, I had lost a husband, a home, my financial security, my health, and I was about to lose my dogs. The devastation was so complete, it was impossible to survey the wreckage in one visual sweep.

What I did have stood in relief against the flattened plain of my former life. I had amazing family and friends who were determined that I would not be leveled too. When you lose everything, you take nothing for granted.

The "Dear John" letter took on a different quality with this new information. I read it again with fresh eyes. I had no idea how many times I would reinterpret the letter as new intelligence was discovered.

"Dear John" letter – Second Interpretation (July 15,2009)

Lisa, I'm afraid there is no easy way for me to say this – I'm leaving. *Yeah, and now I see why. I guess it is kinda hard to stay when the creditors are knock, knock, knockin' at your door.* We have had a long and rich life together but I can no longer live this life anymore. *Is that because you can't afford it after paying for your honey and whatever else you spent OUR money on?* As I told you several months ago, I feel as though we have been drifting apart for a number of years. *You mean to say you have been stealing from me and lying to me for a number of years. I can see how you could confuse that with "drifting."* It was a gradual thing but I can honestly say that it has reached a point where I no longer can share time with you without wondering when I can be away from you again. *Would that be because it is too hard to face me when you have to keep up the lie? I'm sure it was more comfortable to be away from me, not having to see my face when I realized the truth.* I can't keep living this lie – it's not fair to either one of us. *Oh my God, you can tell the truth!* I will continue to support you as best I can from wherever I end up. *Uhh…continue to support me? That would imply that you had been*

47

supporting me. I'm afraid, dear one, that all of the evidence points to the contrary. I will support myself, thank you very much. I will continue to work for DS but I would appreciate if you didn't involve them in this matter. *What, you don't want them to know that you have no boundaries with money? Reason for promotion: Timothy is exceptional at covering financial deceptions and draining accounts with no evidence of spending left behind. He is a self-starter, and is entirely self-taught. He is highly motivated to manipulate and is ruthless in his dealings with others. He is wonderful at pretending to be a team player, and can pull the wool over anyone's eyes.* We had some amazing times together and I will treasure these memories for the rest of my life. *Which wouldn't be very long if I could get my hands on you. I think I would start the process with circumcision by paper cut.* I think people change as they experience life and unfortunately we have grown so far apart that I simply cannot relate to you in any way. *I would sure say that this is pretty far.* I know that this will hit you very hard and for that I am sincerely sorry. *Are you really? Is that why you left me to clean up your shit?*

I have never wanted to do anything to harm you in any way but in doing so I have made myself unhappy for many years. *I'm glad to hear that lying to me did not bring you joy and peace.* I know that once you recover from the shock of this you will bounce back and live a happy and satisfying life – a better and more honest life than I could ever hope to offer you. *Oh, certainly more honest than what you were giving me.* Everything I have left behind is yours and all I have taken is my clothing and the equipment I need to make a living. *...and all the money. I guess you forgot to mention that one.* I will never ask you for forgiveness or understanding. *Good, because they are in even shorter supply than money.* I am a coward who couldn't tell you to your face that I am leaving. *Would that be because you were having Lorena Bobbit dreams when you pictured my finding out about the money and the affair while in your presence? I hope they still haunt your sleep.* If I don't do this now then I probably never will. *What would you do then? This was eminent. Would I have come home to a Fisher-Price sandbox and your head buried up to the neck? You certainly did not leave yourself many options.* I need my life to have some sort of meaning to it and unfortunately working in the basement of my house and watching tv and playing video games isn't it. *Meaning?*

I'm sorry but my life is very quickly becoming that of my parents. *Do you mean because they sucked with money too?* No matter how much I see that, it feels like there is nothing I can do to change the path that I am on.

Another truth! Careful, you might sprain your conscience. From this point on there is nothing more that I can say other than how sorry I am for leaving you in this way. ***Do you mean the text, the affair, the debt? Which are you sorry for? All of it? Any of it?*** I will do everything I can from this point forward to try and make this as easy on you as possible. ***Again, I feel like you are confused. Panicked trips to the mailbox are not easy. Seeing purchases for another woman is not easy. Facing bankruptcy is not easy. Receiving no response from you is not easy. Calling creditors is not easy. Staying in this house is not easy. Breathing is not easy. Maybe you need a dictionary.*** I didn't strip the account to leave. ***What do I say to this? Was this a technicality? It is true, you stripped them prior to your leaving, but you still stripped them.*** I sold everything downstairs that I felt was part of the old me that I so desperately need to leave behind. ***Ah, did you*** sell ***the financial records, then?***

Lesson Three

You are stronger and more resilient than you ever thought you could be.

I was beginning to feel like Marlow on the great river as my own heart filled with darkness at the realization of the brutality my husband was capable of. I had been like the Europeans, turning a blind eye to the horror in the depths of the Congo as colonialization made its march across the continent. Like Marlow, I needed to see the truth hidden in the darkness while avoiding being consumed by it like my husband or the power-hungry Kurtz who did not see the horror until it was too late.

May 2009

I searched through my memories, looking for signs in the rearview mirror. What warning signs did I miss or misinterpret? Indicators that something was amiss only began to arrive that spring, just over three months before he disappeared. By the time the signs were visible, the brake line had already been cut and the crash was imminent.

One particular night stood out.

I began to sense a distance between us in late April of 2009. It was nothing major. It was just the normal hiccup experienced in any longer term relationship when life gets in the way. I initiated a conversation with him one night in early May. We lay on the bed ensconced in each other's arms throughout the five-hour palaver.

My instinct was that we were distancing because we had both been too focused on work, and not on each other and the relationship. This would not be a first for us; we both work hard and gain satisfaction through professional successes, and at times at the expense of personal relationships. I was at the tail end of a very challenging and frustrating school year and Timothy was in the first couple months of a new job that had him working from home and he had been traveling extensively. There was no secret that we needed to regain some balance in our lives.

I was stunned when he mentioned that he was not happy.

My initial reaction was that he might be depressed; he could not clarify why he was not happy – work, marriage, or life in general. Much of that night passed in a blur, but one thirty-minute episode is etched forever in my mind.

He broke down.

His harsh, jagged cries shook the four-poster king-sized bed, rattling it against the floor.

His breath was uneven, his wails primal.

He repeated the same words over and over.

"I'm so sorry."

Heaving inhale. His shrill keening awoke the slumbering dogs.

"I'm so sorry I failed you."

Convulsive sobs. Shuddering exhale.

Repeat.

I wish I had known what he meant at the time.

He let the truth slip through that night.

He never let it out again.

After his crying settled, I reassured him that my job at the time was to be supportive, but not push him. He needed to take some time to focus on himself, starting with his physical health. He had always been healthy, but hypertension had slipped in and became extremely severe in the last couple months. Timothy had actually passed out in March at a trade show in Las Vegas, and again after a doctor's appointment in Atlanta in May. The first doctor he saw after Las Vegas prescribed two different hypertension medications which proved to be useless. He also noted the presence of a sinus arrhythmia and suggested there may be an underlying neurological condition. On this May evening, Timothy was a few days away from meeting with an endocrinologist who would order a large battery of blood and urine tests. He said that his mental anguish was due to the stress of the hypertension and its unknown causes and potentially serious repercussions. I believed him.

It was a chicken and egg riddle, and I made the wrong guess. I suspect now that his blood was the mercury in the barometer of his lies.

Shortly after his anguish was released, Timothy fell asleep. I could not sleep. I was panicked. I was concerned for him. I even asked if I needed to worry about him hurting himself. I was scared for the marriage; was this to be the end? I could not picture life without him. I was desperate to help him; I hated to see him in pain, to see him unhappy.

He never mentioned divorce or separation. Then or ever.

As Timothy slept, I moved to my office to begin to look for help for him. I knew that he (and we) could not do this alone. I navigated through the insurance web pages, and compiled a list of psychologists and counselors in our area. Therapy required that he call in for pre-approval; I had the phone number and directions for approval written at the top of the provider list. I located a checklist of symptoms for clinical depression and included that, too.

I needed some action so that I could maintain hope that he would be okay, that we would be okay.

The next day at work, I was hardly able to function due to anxiety and lack of rest. I had images flashing through my head of a life without Timothy. They were foreign. They were painful. They were unwelcome. They were impossible to ignore.

Hope and disappointment collided the night after his break-down. Timothy was very affectionate and loving, but he had taken no action. The list of therapists had been moved to his office where it sat untouched.

I continued from my place of action.

I wanted to let him know how much I adored him and I wanted him to hear all of the little things I loved about him. I wanted him to know he was valued, appreciated, respected. Excited, I sat up one night and wrote dozens of phrases, tidbits of love, on slips of cream-colored paper. I filled a blue vase with the slips and sat it on the kitchen island with directions for him to draw three slips once he awoke that day. I also left green slips with directions for him to write to me. I left for work with a smile on my face and in my heart, and hoped that he would treasure reading them as much as I did writing them.

They were untouched when I got home.

Instead of letting myself get upset about his lack of participation, I simply grabbed three slips and put them in his hand.

He read them aloud.

He smiled.

He reached for me.

My disappointment erased, I relaxed into his arms.

I initiated several more conversations that week. He was always willing to talk, even thanking me for waking him one morning before I left so that I did not leave the house upset. I was scared for him. I was anxious about the future. I was angry that he had kept this from me. We talked, I cried, and we held on to each other as we talked. He was gentle, affirming, loving.

I continued to write more slips at a manic pace. Opened slips poured off the top of the microwave like autumn leaves until I retrieved an envelope to contain them. He always seemed to enjoy reading them and I loved writing them.

I love the moment your kisses turn from gentle to passionate.

I love how have been able to teach yourself so much.

I love how trustworthy you are.

I love that we have shared so many things together.

Throughout, our focus remained on his physical health. We were both scared. His blood pressure was uncontrolled, and he frequently felt very ill and dizzy.

The green slips remained blank.

After several days with no action, I threw the green slips in the garbage. They were too painful to look at. I was sobbing quietly as I went into the master bath to brush my teeth. Timothy awoke to my cries and immediately cradled me, soothed me. He apologized for being remiss about filling out the slips and was disheartened that I threw them away. He asked me to cut new ones and promised that he would complete them.

He kept his promise.

I love that you go after what you want.

I love that I can bounce a quarter off your ass.

I love that we share so much together.

I love watching you solve problems.

The vase became half cream and half green.

On the day after I returned from Seattle, I burned all the slips of paper - all the proclamations of love.

They disappeared, leaving no residue, as if they were never there.

The visit with the endocrinologist came and went, and lab results were still a few weeks away. He seemed happier and we settled back into some sense of normalcy, still very aware of the medical information that could change everything. I didn't push too hard, for I saw him as fragile at that point. Cracks formed by the surging pressure in his veins.

He was so good at soothing me, reassuring me, and holding me. I wanted to believe in his words that May, and so I did. He told me how much he loved me. I listened. He made love to me. I melted. He told me he was sorry for scaring me. I trusted. Desire shapes belief.

We continued on with life. We went to an outdoor showing of E.T., and had to leave early because we could not keep our hands off each other. An indoor movie didn't fare any better; we never even made it out of the parking lot. We read, intertwined on the sofa as was our custom. We spent warm summer days on the deck and warm summer evenings watching movies. We planned the rest of my time off, and discussed our future.

Just as the school year drew to a close, he announced he had a business trip to Brazil for two weeks in June. I was scared. I was worried for him and did not want him out of the country while his health was in the balance. My anxiety was not misplaced, but it had the wrong target. His health was not what I needed to be concerned about.

This job was to be supervising an install for Jaguar at a large auto show in Rio de Janerio. Ford Auto Group had been a major client of his for several years and he frequently had to go on site for major shows. He had always done quite a bit (too much) travel for work and international travel was not unusual. In the weeks leading up to the trip, he mentioned that his company was absorbing the costs associated with securing a new passport and a Brazilian visa, using an expediting service. He talked about the job, the on site project manager, and his fears based on the lack of specifications for the facility and the language barrier. I was dreading the trip as I was still uneasy due to the events of the months before, but I never doubted its veracity. I had no reason to.

June 2009

Brazil. I received the following from him while he was running errands before the trip and waiting at the Atlanta airport.

Mr T   6/12/09   2:22 p.m.

"I love you! Big big"

Mr T   6/12/09   2:46 p.m.

"I'll be back before you know it!"

Mr T   6/12/09   5:05 pm

"...Let's look at dates when I get back to see what might work. Love ya!"

This related to a coast trip that I had spent that afternoon planning. We were looking at the weekend of July 18 or 25 and I was excited to finally spend a day with Timothy at the Georgia coast.

While he spent his first week in Brazil, I spent some of my time recuperating from an injury while easing back into running. I had not planned to do any work for school that month, but I decided that it would be a wise use of my days. Time passed easily.

Mr T   6/16/09   5:35 p.m.

"I miss you terribly! This is a very different and strange place – I can't wait to tell you about it. I hope you're doing well – love you!"

This was my first contact with him since a call when he landed. Sporadic contact while out of town had always been normal, especially with international trips. I didn't think anything of it; I had always trusted Timothy completely. I hated his travel, but had long ago accepted it as part of our lives.

Three days later.

Mr T   6/19/09   3:57 p.m.

"I miss you! Hope you're doing ok – I'll try to call this weekend if I can. Love you!"

and

Mr T   6/19/09   6:34 p.m.

"I really wish I was going home sooner…Brazilians can't make their mind up worth a crap! I love you and hope you're doing ok. Be well."

These messages were the highlight of my days. I still felt a flutter in my stomach when I saw "Mr. T" on the phone display after many years. Yeah, corny, I know.

The second week in Brazil was not as smooth as the first. On the twenty-third, I received two items in the mail that first allowed the worm of doubt to enter my brain. As the worm fed on the information contained within the envelopes, it secreted anxiety which soon overwhelmed my body. Not wanting to bother Timothy in Brazil, I went down to his office to see if I could locate any information to sooth my fears or at least to explain them.

The door was locked.

The door was never locked.

I checked the basket by the microwave for the key.

Missing.

The worm grew.

After finding the door locked, I was no longer concerned about bothering Timothy in Brazil. I texted him and left a voice message, letting him know that it was urgent that I talk to him. He called back promptly. I asked him about the Best Buy letter that indicated a balance of $9,000.00 (about $8,000.00 more than I was aware of) and was threatening action since the account had not been paid in months. Timothy acted surprised, but mainly annoyed that the company had screwed up. I asked him about the second notice from the IRS. He reassured me that he had written them after the first notice, contesting the charge. I questioned him about the locked door. He said that it must have accidentally locked (this did happen to that particular door occasionally) and that he thought the key was in the basket. My anxiety dropped from a 10 to an eight after talking to him, but the worm was still restless.

I think he knew my trust was uneasy.

Mr T   6/23/09   12:04 p.m.

"I can't get a signal for more than a few seconds right now...I'll walk around tonight to try and find something that works. Don't worry – everything's fine! Love you and miss the crap out of you!"

Mr T   6/23/09   12:38 p.m.

"No prob bob! Sorry for the scare – whatever that is I'll dig into it when I get home. Love you big big!!!"

Mr T   6/24/09   12:31 p.m.

"I can't get away to call right now and these messages take four or five tries to send. I pay the bill [Best Buy] every month on the ninth and then I watch it get deducted from the account every month. I don't get paper bills and I have payment confirmations dating back years. I'm not sure what else I can tell you right now. I will call tonight if I can get away before it's too late."

The anxiety lessened a little more. I wanted to believe him; I had no reason not to trust him.

Mr T   6/25/09   7:00 a.m.

"Can't talk very bad food poisoning throwing up all night as bad as January call when I can love you"

I ached for him, I wished I could help. The food poisoning in January knocked us both down for a week, and almost resulted in dual hospital stays. He was alone. In pain. As the next few days passed and I did not hear from, my anxiety was for his health. I did not sleep. I did not eat. My only clarity came from my daily run. The rest was obsessive fear. The worst event I could ever imagine was losing him, and I was petrified that he would not survive the trip.

The text about the food poisoning came in the day after I called him about a letter from the power company stating that the bill had not been paid.

He was supposed to return to Atlanta on June 30. The flight was to land at 6:00 in the morning.

I waited until 7:15 to call him, allowing time for him to move through customs.

No answer.

Panic.

Two hours. Pacing. Trembling. Overwhelming fear engulfed me. Was this it? Was he gone? The trepidation had been building all week, and this sent it over the edge.

I located the number for the U.S. Embassy, but I was shaking too much to call.

At 10:00 a.m., I finally called his boss at the company headquarters in Detroit. I said that I had expected Timothy to return that morning and I had not heard from him. His boss sounded puzzled, but said he would check and get back to me.

Mr T   6/30/09   10:19 a.m.

"I leave today love and get back early tomorrow morning. If I can find a good cell spot then I'll give you a call otherwise I will be racing home to you can't wait to get back to see you. Love you!!!"

Breath.

Trembling eased.

There was pure unbridled joy when he walked into the house on July 1. It felt so amazing to hold him, kiss him, smell him, feel his heat. We had only a few short days together before I was to leave for Seattle on the morning of the fifth. I was determined to make the best of them.

On his first afternoon home, I brought up the strange bills (now numbering four) that came in while he was in Brazil. He was calm. He held me and said that he would look into it, take care of it, and that everything would be okay.

Looking into his eyes,

"Please be completely honest with me. I need to know if there is anything financially that I need to know, anything that you're keeping from me."

Holding me tight, cradling my head,

"I promise that everything is okay. I'm sorry that this scared you. Everything is fine. I have been busy with work and not feeling well. I'll double-check and make sure nothing is slipping through."

Pulling back slightly, I said, "Why don't you take care of it this next week, get it straightened out. Then, when I get back, I want to look at finances together. We have not done that in a while, and I want to make sure that we are still on the same page."

Hugging me close again, "That sounds like a good idea."

The worm had been soothed, but not killed. It continued to stir, and left doubts in its wake.

The days between Brazil and my trip to Seattle passed in a happy blur. Errands. Dinners. Sex. A fireworks show to celebrate the fourth. We planned a trip to the coast when I returned. We discussed plans for August weekends. We lived. We loved.

July 20, 2009

My journal that day reflected my anger as I realized his texts while in Brazil were designed to pacify me like the captive humans in *The Matrix*, so that he could continue to feed off of me a little longer. The bold strokes that formed the words that poured out of me that day wore deep grooves in the paper.

> *"You tried to get my sympathy – sick in Brazil? – while fucking her. I fell for it. I felt so bad for you. Scared for you. You never thought of me. There are no words that describe how despicable you are. I can't believe you texted me lovey-dovies while you were with her. Did you laugh at that? You are the fool. At least I don't have to run from myself. The rage I feel is powerful and could cut you down. You are wise to stay away."*

One recent incident gained clarity as I realized the dark financial undercurrent of our lives. Just before I left for Seattle on July 2, Timothy came upstairs from his office, grumbling about "fucking Toyota." He stated that there was a mistake when he made the electronic car payment. The claim was that the computer deducted 10 months of payments instead of a single month. He explained that this wiped out the checking and savings accounts (this would correspond with the amount of money I anticipated in the accounts.)

I asked for an update 30 minutes later.

Mr T   7/2/09 10:42 am

Nothing good. I've talked to a couple of layers and I'm now back to waiting for another call-back from their online payment division. To make matters worse this isn't officially a Toyota issue but swtf-which is the company who financed the loan. I've also talked to USAA but they can't do anything until the payment moves from pending to posted. Wheeeeeeeee

This meant that I was heading to Seattle with only the $100 taken from an ATM on July 1 to my name. At least I knew there would be money available on July 7, when his paycheck posted.

However, when I tried to pay for lunch in Seattle on the ninth, my card did not go through. I texted this to him. He replied with the following:

Mr T   7/9/09 3:22 pm

Damn it. I'm sick and tired of this. The check from Toyota has a hold on it until Monday, but the balance on the account shows it only as pending. So I thought the check was in and paid our bills...the long and short of it is that we're right back where we were just a few days ago because of fucking SE Toyota again.

It came as no surprise that, in pursuing the checking account activity several days later, the car payment was deducted normally. I had no money, not because of a snafu with a finance company, but because my husband deliberately spent it on another woman. Somehow those don't quite have the same flavor.

July 5, 2009

When he walked to airport security to send me off on my Seattle trip, he gave me a long hug. Several deep kisses. Held me close.

"The week will pass quickly. You'll be back before you know it and we'll have lots of time together. And, unlike Brazil, we can keep in constant contact."

He started the contact almost immediately.

Mr T   7/5/09   6:49 am

Love ya!!! Have a smooth flight and be safe!

Mr T   7/5/09 7:41 am

I told ya I'd stay in touch!

Mr T   7/5/09 3:05 pm

Love you!!!

Mr T   7/5/09 3:08 pm

Welcome to Seattle!

Life was normal from my perspective. Meanwhile, the man I thought was my partner was actually my Judas, planning my demise.

July 19, 2009

My dad left. My mom arrived. The changing of the guard.

We thought the worst was behind us.

We thought it was time to focus on pursuing the steps already initiated.

We thought we could take the first tentative steps on the road towards healing.

We were wrong.

My mom took over the task of trying to locate homes for the dogs, beginning with calling Janet, a friend of mine from work that I had alerted to the situation. While my mom worked the phone, I wrote descriptions of my three dogs to be used to find the best possible homes for them.

Max (pug) – 13 years

Max has been with me since she was seven weeks old. From day one, she was smart and spunky and made sure that her presence was always known. As an only dog for four years, she was very spoiled. Her intelligence has always been impressive – she used to know the names of about 10 individual toys. She has never been afraid of new experiences; she earned the nickname "all terrain pug" for her willingness to tackle challenging hikes.

She gets along well with the two other dogs and the cat. She is the dominant one, although the others have been challenging her lately as her age limits her ability to defend her throne.

67

Like many pugs, she sometimes has allergy problems, although hers have been limited to contact dermatitis. She is still quite mobile, even with some arthritis in her front left shoulder. Her hearing and vision are poor at this point; she responds better to visual clues than verbal. She has been on Science Diet SO4 for several years due to repeated urinary tract infections. She was due a few weeks ago for a vet/vaccine visit, but I have been unable to take her.

Max loves to destroy stuffed animals and loves to chew (or gum) bones. She tends to spend extended time in the backyard exploring and sniffing around. She likes nothing more than a good butt or belly scratch.

Porter (Boston terrier) – 9 years

Porter also joined the family as a young puppy. He has always been super affectionate and loves attention. He had a spiral fracture of the femur when he was 6 months old. The break was treated with internal fixation and the rod was removed several months later. He completely recovered physically from the break, but it left him a little fearful of new situations. He does well with other people and dogs, but he needs some patience and supervision at the beginning to help him overcome his fear of the unknown. He is super loving and enjoys being held and giving sloppy kisses.

We have always called Porter our "special child" due to his idiosyncrasies. He is very spatially intelligent and uses his understanding of his environment to manipulate objects around him. He can frequently be found behind a closed door because he uses his paws and face to shut the door behind him. Upon waking, you may find that he has rearranged a piece of furniture to his liking. He spends some of his down time "nursing" on tennis balls and other similar toys. He frequently plays with the other dogs in the house.

Porter's health has been excellent. He is up to date on his vaccines. He has never been a good eater, and he often requests some loving to "jump start" him.

Porter had a special bond with my soon to be ex husband and has shown signs of distress since he left. He is very sensitive and will need some extra love to help him in this difficult time.

Glottis (lab/border collie mix) – Six years

Glottis was adopted into the family when she was a young puppy. From day one, she was an absolute joy; a fun, happy-go-lucky dog that loved everyone and everything. She has amazing talents with tennis balls – she will hold one in her mouth and bat another one around the house with her paws. She also loves to play fetch and is excellent at returning the ball. She loves to play with other dogs and is very friendly with her feline sibling.

Glottis is in excellent health and her vaccines are current. She has put on a few pounds due to the stresses of the last couple of weeks, but has previously been a steady and healthy weight.

Glottis is very tuned in to those around her and she gives great hugs when you've had a bad day. She is always ready for attention and especially loves to have her belly and her ears scratched. She is simply an all-around amazing companion.

All three descriptions concluded with the following:

I never thought that I would have to surrender my beloved dogs, but I am forced to as my husband left me abruptly with no home and no money. This decision is devastating for me; however, I know that I cannot give the dogs the care, attention, and love they need at this time. I want them to be in a loving environment where they can thrive and they can share their gifts with others. Thank you for helping to ensure that they have a good future.

We began to send the letters off to promising leads.

Now that steps were taken towards the dog's well-being, it was time to look after my health. I had scheduled an appointment with my gynecologist soon after returning to Atlanta. I had not needed my mom in the exam room with me since I was 14. I needed her now. I was petrified that I may have contracted an STD (or several) from Timothy since we had not used condoms for over ten years and remained sexually active until I left for Seattle.

I sat in the waiting room, my body rigid, curled into a semi-fetal position. My forever shaking leg clattered against the frame of the chair. When called, I shuffled to the exam room and disrobed. My mom gasped when she saw the gauntness of my frame; my ribs stood out in relief along my back. Pulling on the paper gown, I sat shivering and shaking on the edge of the exam table. The doctor commented on my thinness as she noted my protruding hips. She indicated that action would need to be taken if I did not start to eat soon.

My urine sample was dusky pink with blood as my body broke down muscle tissue to try to fuel its critical processes. My electrolytes were depressed as if reading my mind. I had developed an arrhythmia triggered by the breaking down of cardiac tissue and the lowered potassium in my blood. If I didn't start to eat soon, I would literally be dying of a broken heart.

This was unlike any pelvic exam I had ever had. I had never before worried about what may be found. I was numb to what was normally an uncomfortable procedure; all my pain was in my head. Sitting up, I had to steady myself as the room began to swim. My body was at the breaking point, but it still had further to go as I had to have blood drawn to test for any possible diseases that would not allow the July disaster to fade into the past: HIV and hepatitis. I watched the blood swirl into the vial, questioning its contents.

I left the doctor's office not knowing what secrets my body held. I hoped that I could recover emotionally and financially from his deceptions, but did his actions leave me with inescapable physical consequences?

With the doctor appointment behind me and the wait for results ahead, we focused on building the foundation of my new life. I had a place to live. I obtained a gym membership since I had lost my home gym. I purchased some gym clothes because I could no longer work out in my underwear. I bought a Costco membership in my name. I found a new "signature scent," leaving my old perfumes as relics in the abandoned house. I investigated signing up for a marathon or half-marathon. I downloaded the information for a AAA membership.

The pieces were being collected and assembled that would begin to represent a new life - a future. Unfortunately, it still resembled a landscape painted by Salvador Dali: the surreal in sharp contrast to the common.

Throughout the forays into the future, I monitored the joint checking account. By using triangulation of debits and ATM withdrawals, I was able to determine that Timothy was staying in the Ames, Iowa area. We did not know anyone in Iowa; he had no legitimate business there. I concluded that he was there with *her*, the mystery woman he was with in Brazil. I found it amusing that in trying to escape the "dull" life in an Atlanta suburb, he ended up in the cornfields of the Midwest.

I also learned from the account that several of his "business" trips over the preceding months had been to Iowa, at a cost of over $1,000.00 a piece. No wonder he was having trouble paying Best Buy.

I had enough information that I could have pursued to find out who she was and where they were. I made a conscious effort not to move that direction; he was gone and apparently wanted to stay gone. Besides, after uncovering his deceit, I was ready to hand him over to her. I never did find lies and betrayal to be an aphrodisiac.

There was peace in the ambiguity. I could proceed with a no-fault divorce by publication. Hope that my blood tests were clear. Wipe the financial slate clean with a bankruptcy. And move forward without having to carefully examine the wounds. I wanted to look forward through the windshield of my life, and not focus in the rearview mirror at the destruction that lay behind me, questioning its causes and mechanisms.

That changed on July 20; I discovered the following message resting amongst the spam in his junk mail:

Did I send this to you already? if not, here it is (for the visa app).

Love ya,

Amanda

----- Forwarded Message ----

>*Sent: Thursday, July 16, 2009 12:48:32 AM*
>
>*Subject: Re: phone number?*
>
>*Sure!*
>
>*Let me know if you need a physical address or PO Box!*
>
>*Cheers,*
>
>*On Thu, Jul 16, 2009 at 6:19 AM, Amanda wrote:*

Hey,

The Uganda visa application asks for a contact within Uganda - do you have a phone number I could put for you?

Thanks!!

Amanda

PhD candidate, Geography

Iowa State

Don't wait for strangers to remind you of your duty,
you have a conscience and a spirit for that.
All the good you do must come from your own initiative.
-Popul Vuh

Uganda?

As in Africa?

That certainly added some spice. I had to giggle a bit at the thought of a man who was nervous in the tourist areas of Jamaica going to Africa. He was too accustomed to the comforts of suburban life to be able to make it in an African village. I pictured him in his Banana Republic sweater, iPhone in hand, walking down a dirt road shared with goats. I envisioned him trying in vain to find consistent internet access for his multiple Macintoshes. I smiled at the thought of him trying to order a hamburger or his favorite domestic brew. I wondered why Uganda. It struck me that it was a good place to hide.

Friends and family began to joke about sending him some care packages; we did not want him to suffer too much while he was away from the comforts of home. We had fun debating the proper contents of the box. We finally settled on mosquito attractant, non-alcoholic beer, and itchy wool socks impregnated with fire ant eggs along with other items to remind him of home

It took me a few moments to realize that I now had a name, employer, and e-mail address for her. It took more than that to determine what I wanted to do with this information.

I had not tried to contact Timothy in eight days. I could feel my anxiety building as I held in the words I needed him to hear. Since he had robbed me of my opportunity to talk *with* him, I decided to try for another e-mail. This time, I included Amanda in the recipient list.

Amanda-

I do not feel the need to involve you in this. I do not know what Timothy has told you about our life and marriage, but I know that you cannot be entirely in the dark about his past after being in the house. You have made your decisions consciously.

Please make sure that he gets the message below, as I'm not sure that he is checking his MMS account. Lisa

Timothy-

Uganda is an interesting choice.

You were right about two things: you are a coward and you certainly did let me down.

You can never run away from who you are or the knowledge of what you have done. Even Africa is not far enough.

I wonder how long it will take Amanda to see you for what you are?

You have taken away 16 years of my life, my dogs (true innocents whose lives are now completely changed), my home, my financial security, and what I thought was a wonderful marriage. You stole my youth, my innocence, my love. You hurt me in the ways in which you knew I was the most vulnerable. I refuse to let you have any more.

At least I can be at peace with who I am and the decisions that I have made.

I will not attempt to contact you again unless I find out this week that I have contracted an STD from you. That would be one more thing to weigh on your conscience.

Your betrayal and lies have pierced me to the core. I have never felt such pain, such sadness, such anger. The one I trusted and adored deceived and abandoned me.

Lisa

Within minutes of sending the letter, the password on my e-mail had changed and I was unable to access my account. I knew then that he had received my message.

I had always seen myself as a survivor. I knew I was tough. I wasn't sure, however, that was enough to see me through to the end of this nightmare. I was facing the fact that I was physically afraid of my husband for the first time ever. My mom and I changed the locks and disabled the garage door so that he could not enter the house unannounced while my mom still slept there with the dogs. We notified the police of the situation, hoping to file a restraining order. They wouldn't issue the order, but upon hearing the story commented that I was lucky to escape alive. They did offer to keep an eye on the house for us. We gratefully accepted just in case this particular devil made his way back down to Georgia.

I had so many questions. I was trying to perform a marital autopsy with no body, a postmortem non corpus. But all I could think about at that moment was staying upright and moving forward. I wasn't sure how I was going to weather this storm, but I was learning that my roots were stronger than I realized.

As I recorded in my journal on July 16,

"I think he expected me to stay in fear and collapse. I need to show him (and me) the power I can have to move forward and beyond. He has taken so much from me, but he can't take me."

"Dear John" letter – Third Interpretation (July 20, 2009)

Lisa,

I'm afraid there is no easy way for me to say this – I'm leaving. *I think Atlanta to Africa certainly qualifies as leaving.* We have had a long and rich life together but I can no longer live this life anymore. *A life as an American?* As I told you several months ago, I feel as though we have been drifting apart for a number of years. *More like you running away.* It was a gradual thing but I can honestly say that it has reached a point where I no longer can share time with you without wondering when I can be away from you again. *Looks like you won't need to worry about that anymore – I don't think I'll be bumping into you at the grocery store.* I can't keep living this lie – it's not fair to either one of us. *How long have you been planning this? I would have noticed "Uganda: the Place for Lovers" brochures in the mail.* I will continue to support you as best I can from wherever I end up. *It sounds like you knew the "wherever."* I will continue to work for DS but I would appreciate if you didn't involve them in this matter. *I didn't realize that DS had a Ugandan office.* We had some amazing times together and I will treasure these memories for the rest of my life. *However long that may be...Uganda is not the safest place.* I think people

78

change as they experience life and unfortunately we have grown so far apart that I simply cannot relate to you in any way. *Apparently, I can't relate to you either. I never saw you for the "move to Africa" type.* I know that this will hit you very hard and for that I am sincerely sorry. *Your actions thus far have not shown any remorse. You have made no attempt to contact me or even to see if I am okay. I do believe that you are sincerely self-centered.* I have never wanted to do anything to harm you in any way but in doing so I have made myself unhappy for many years. *Since when is my happiness and yours mutually exclusive?* I know that once you recover from the shock of this you will bounce back and live a happy and satisfying life – a better and more honest life than I could ever hope to offer you. *What is the standard recovery time for a shock of this magnitude, I wonder?* Everything I have left behind is yours and all I have taken is my clothing and the equipment I need to make a living. *You left the bug spray. Too bad. You may have found that helpful in Uganda.*

I will never ask you for forgiveness or understanding. *What are you asking me for, then? A blind eye?* I am a coward who couldn't tell you to your face that I am leaving. *...and who couldn't face the repercussions of his decisions.* If I don't do this now then I probably never will. *True. The window to get a free ride to Uganda is* *rather narrow. I wonder if the promise of a place to run to is what drew you to Amanda in the first place?* I need my life to have some sort of meaning to it and unfortunately working in the basement of my house and watching tv and playing video games isn't it. *Well, you won't have to worry about that in Uganda. I doubt they have basements.*

I'm sorry but my life is very quickly becoming that of my parents. *This decision certainly changes that.* No matter how much I see that, it feels like there is nothing I can do to change the path that I am on. *What path? The yellow brick road away from your problems?* From this point on there is nothing more that I can say other than how sorry I am for leaving you in this way. *This most definitely qualifies as abandonment, now.* I will do everything I can from this point forward to try and make this as easy on you as possible. *Disappearing from the country is not making things easy.* I didn't strip the account to leave. *Only because it was already pre-stripped.* I sold everything downstairs that I felt was part of the old me that I so desperately need to leave behind. *Did you sell the Toyota, too? I don't think you'll need it in Uganda.*

Lesson Four

Laughter and tears are only separated by a thin veil.

The dark humor began to take hold. My mom and I were sleep deprived and I was still not eating, both conditions conducive to giggling. We began to find hilarity in the strangest places like stoned college students trying to have an all-night study session. The reality was stranger than any pipe dream I could imagine. Each day only brought more absurdity. I felt like I was trapped in a world imagined by Jerry Springer and carried out by Roger Rabbit. I had traveled into the Twilight Zone and there was no telling just how crazy it was going to get.

When I first discovered evidence of an affair, I intentionally decided not to dig too deep, to try to discover who she was. It was too painful and did not seem to serve any purpose. Additionally, the affair was simply one of a long list of betrayals and its pain was inseparable from the other transgressions with only the added fear of disease. Who knew that Darwin's survival of the fittest theory extended to breaches of trust?

The Uganda e-mail changed that. Now I had a name. A job. A picture. A life. She became real.

Images of the two of them together now flashed unwelcomed through my mind. The strange details I had noticed in the house

81

pushed their way to the forefront of my mind. Now I saw Amanda in my space, drinking wine, wrapping herself in my sheets and drying her naked flesh on my guest towels. I wondered what stories he told her? How he explained my clothes? The slips of paper? She must have known that I was still very much in the picture.

As the reality of Amanda obtained hold, Brazil gained texture, and lost some of its abstract protective coating. Exposed thought surfaces began to rust and I started to perceive the recent past differently, and began to comprehend the cruelty and deliberateness of his actions. The charges on the accounts became tangible; these were real places visited with a real woman. This actually happened.

My mind began to fixate. Amanda had an active internet presence and I explored every blog and examined every picture, trying to get a better sense of her. Who was this woman that was so attractive to him? What was it about her that drew him away from me? She seemed entrenched in academia, a world with which he was not familiar nor comfortable. She appeared to be a free spirit, never settling in one place for long, as opposed to Timothy's reluctance towards the new. Her passions were tied to social causes, never an interest of Timothy's. I did not understand. Did he like her for the freedoms that she represented? The escape she could provide in Uganda? Or was it deeper?

July 2009

The night that carried July 21 into the 22 was a long one. My journal, which had lifted away some of my grief and anger the preceding few days, grew lax at its job. I was raged. How could he do this and not allow me the opportunity to speak? I realized that the first e-mail I sent to him was too restrained, too civilized. I did not want to become vindictive, but I also felt no need to protect his delicate sensibilities. I sat down at the computer to write and the words poured forth uncensored.

I called my mom, who was at the old house with the dogs, at around 3:00 a.m. to have her read the e-mail before I sent it. I expected caution, advice that this should be written, not sent. Advice that should it be given, would remain unheeded as I could tell that *I* needed this to be read by him.

She gave her blessing for me to send it and I quickly complied, again adding Amanda to the recipient list.

July 22, 2009   3:25 a.m.

Timothy-

I do not have the STD results yet. I figure you will be gone by the time I know my fate. You know your risks.

You were right.

You were right. I will never understand. I will never understand how you could be so cruel to someone you once loved. How you could repeatedly lie, even to direct questions for many months and years. How you could say goodbye at the airport, knowing it was for good, yet telling me that the week would go quickly and we would see each other soon. How you could continue to act like everything was okay (making plans for the future, sending loving texts, saying you missed me, having sex, even putting your fucking dirty clothes in the basket before you left town), all the while knowing what you had done, were doing, and were planning to do. How you could betray my trust: financially, sexually, and in every other way. How you could make me feel sorry for you (sick in Brazil?) while you were fucking your girlfriend all the while and spending thousands of dollars from OUR account? How you could continue to lie in your text (talk to you in a few days) and letter (I didn't drain the account) to string me along as long as possible. Every piece I find out is a knife right through the gut (and trust me, I have found out quite a lot). The pain you saw me in 2 1/2 months ago is a tiny sliver of what I am feeling now. You not only stole my present, you robbed me of my past: I can no longer look back on any of our relationship with any degree of fondness. Was any of it real? I don't want to understand what you have done because in order to understand I would have to be deceitful and despicable too. I could never do the things you did.

You were right. You are a coward. You still cannot face me, face what you have done. I am left here to try to pick up the pieces of what you ran away from. You have left me with my two biggest fears: losing you (although I always thought it would be to death - that would have been so much easier) and financial ruin. I, however, am facing my fears. That is more than can be said for you.

You were right. I will never forgive you. You could have handled this so many ways, but you managed to do it in the most painful way possible. I used to adore you more than anything else in this world, now I see nothing at all in you that is worthy of love.

You were right. You have failed me. Not only have you failed your vows, you also promised me that you would never lie, never cheat. If you needed out, I would have let you go. You never gave me a chance. You failed the dogs. I am no longer able to care for them physically, emotionally, financially. Glottis and Porter and going to two separate homes on Sunday. We have been unable to find placement for Max; she will most likely be euthanized early next week. Her death rests squarely on your shoulders.

You failed my family. They loved you. And now they have to see me utterly devastated.

You were right. I will certainly be living a more honest life. Of course, I was always honest. I have never lied to you, deceived you, cheated on you, withheld information from you. Even now, I operate from a place of integrity (have you noticed that I have not taken money from your automatically deposited paychecks other than to pay for car insurance?). The difference now is that I am not being lied to any more. I notice that you did not say that you would lead a more honest life. I suppose that it is too late for that.

You were right about so many things, but wrong on many more. You are not turning into your parents. They never hid who they really are. You are wrong to think that you can run away from your past - the house of cards has collapsed and it will follow you. You are wrong to think that this will make you happy. You were wrong thinking that I would continue to fall for your lies. You are wrong thinking that you can block out what you have done - it takes more than shutting me out of your e-mail. You were wrong to block out your feelings that led to this. You were wrong to think that you could handle this on your own. You were wrong to abandon our dogs in the basement and me across the country with no money to return. You were wrong to destroy 16 years with a FUCKING text message. You were wrong to steal money from our accounts - I guess fraud alert doesn't work when it is from within the home. You were wrong to bring her to our home. You were wrong to tell me that you wanted to be together right before Brazil - hah! You were wrong to ask me not to contact your work; I certainly don't owe you any favors. You were wrong to have sex with me, exposing me to unknown risks. You were wrong to seek my sympathy. You were wrong to pretend, to lie, to hide. You were wrong to do this to me.

I feel raped. Violated. Dirty. You have shamed me with your lies and your deeds. I was living with and loving an illusion, carefully crafted to take advantage of my trust. What did I do to deserve this treatment? Love too much, trust too much? The level of cruelty you have shown is astounding. The only word for it is "mindfuck" - from kindness to cruelty, protection to persecution, connection to abandonment. There are no words that adequately describe the vileness of your actions. Everything you have touched is poisoned.

You know what's sad? I still find myself wanting to share things with you.

We were such a good team, a good partnership. Unfortunately, a marriage takes two to make it work and only one to destroy it. You certainly destroyed it, and in the process, destroyed part of me. I will never be able to love or trust as innocently again. You stole that from me.

You cannot rest easy. Your creditors will find you. The IRS will find you. From what I have seen, the law may even find you. You cannot run from your health issues - did you even get your lab results? You won't have health insurance soon. How long will your employers put up with your deceptions? They won't like creditors, lawyers, law enforcement calling them. You better hope Amanda stays put - it seems as though you are going to be rather dependent upon her soon. I wonder what lies you have told her? You have no one else to support you - you have pushed them all away and betrayed their trust. You are alone.

Are you still interested in the devil and angel tattoo? Make sure to leave off the angel - we know who you've been listening to.

My shaking finally subsided, but I was still unable to sleep. Refocused after the Uganda surprise, I decided to spend Friday working on my classroom since school was to start in two short weeks. My intentions were thwarted by the discovery that my classroom had been turned into a textbook storage facility over the summer; my work would have to wait. After tackling a few items on the ever-lengthening to do list, my mom and I returned to Sarah's, where I was going to try to do some school work on the computer. The work I ended up doing had nothing to do with school.

I arrived home to the following e-mail in Timothy's junk mail box.

Thank you, Darling...I love you!

Amanda
PhD candidate, Geography
Iowa State

Don't wait for strangers to remind you of your duty,
you have a conscience and a spirit for that.
All the good you do must come from your own initiative.
-Popul Vuh

From: Timothy

To: The Sunflower Field
Cc: Amanda

Sent: Friday, July 24, 2009 11:35:21 AM
Subject: Re: wedding gig 17th of July

Hi Steph,

Sorry about the mixup! I mailed the check as I was leaving Atlanta to make my trip to Ames for our wedding. Instead of risking another lovely postal snafu would it be alright if I dropped you a check sometime on Monday or Tuesday of this coming week? Please let me know what works the best for you so we can get you taken care of as soon as possible.

Thanks again for making Friday such an amazing and wonderful day!

Timothy

Hi Amanda,

The Sunflower Field has not yet received their check for your wedding. I don't doubt that you all sent it, but it seems to have gotten lost somewhere along the way. Do you remember what address you sent it to? Would you mind sending another one?
Thanks for you understanding!
Steph
From: Amanda

To: The Sunflower Field

Sent: Thursday, July 2, 2009 8:38:33 AM
Subject: Re: wedding gig 17th of July

Hi!
We have a big rented white canopy thing in case it
rains.
Thanks so much for making the PA available for IPOD
music, that really helps.
We will send the check next week.
India Palace is catering the party so the food will be
good too!
Let me know if you have any other questions or
concerns, otherwise see you there!
Thanks,
Amanda

———————————————

Amanda
PhD candidate, Geography
Iowa State

Don't wait for strangers to remind you of your duty,
you have a conscience and a spirit for that.
All the good you do must come from your own initiative.
-Popul Vuh

From: The Sunflower Field

To: Amanda
Sent: Thursday, July 2, 2009 10:19:44 AM
Subject: Re: wedding gig 17th of July

Hi, Amanda

This is Scott from the Sunflower Field...Sure, we can get the PA iPod-ready by 530. I'll get there a little early to set stuff up. We have played a wedding at South Park before, it's very pretty there on a summer night! Looking forward to it! You can send the check made out to "The Sunflower Field" tour address.... Or you can give it to us at the event. Either way works fine.

One question...Do you guys have a big rented tent shelter in case it rains? What is the rain plan?

-- Scott

From: Amanda

To: The Sunflower Field
Sent: Wednesday, July 1, 2009 2:30:28 PM
Subject: wedding gig 17th of July

Hello,
My name is Amanda and I am Jennifer's friend who is

*contracting Sunflower Field on the 17th. I just wanted
to touch base with you about the details. We would like
it if the band could play with the small PA you
mentioned in your e-mail to Jennifer. There is power
hookup there at the gazebo. We are thinking of having
people arrive at 530pm, having a small ceremony at
6pm, and then the band can play one set after the
ceremony (630-715) while people eat and play, and
another 745-830pm after we do the pinata at 715..
Does that sound okay? While people arrive we are
hoping to play a recorded playlist off an IPOD - would
there be a chance of cooking that up to your PA? If not,
we can find some other way of amplifying the recorded
music. Just let me know. Also let me know if the band
needs payment prior to the date, or how we should pay
you.
Thanks,
Amanda*

Amanda

*PhD candidate, Geography
Iowa State*

*Don't wait for strangers to remind you of your duty,
you have a conscience and a spirit for that.
All the good you do must come from your own initiative.
-Popul Vuh*

The first time through I interpreted the e-mail as stating that they were planning on getting married soon. It took three passes to comprehend that they were already married.

Married. My *husband* got married.

I read the series of e-mails several more times, trying to make sense of it all. It was wasted effort; there was no sense to it at all.

After the initial shock faded somewhat, one of my first emotions was a strange feeling of relief; he had done something illegal, something that I could now hold him accountable for and would bring in the criminal system. He had progressed on the scale of bad behavior from despicable to illegal. My mom and I quickly moved into action to have him arrested.

I e-mailed my divorce attorney and notified her of the news.

My mom organized the information we had obtained from the e-mail in Timothy's junk mail box.

I found the phone number for the court in Iowa to verify that a "legal" marriage had occurred.

My mom called the Iowa courts. A marriage license was taken out on July 7 and returned on July 24. He actually did it.

I found the number for the district attorney's office in Iowa looking for advice on the next step.

My mom called the district attorney's office.

The clock was counting down to the end of business hours on Friday afternoon.

I searched local records for evidence of a divorce. If I could procure a divorce by publication without his knowledge, he could have done the same.

My mom talked to a clerk at the district attorney's office.

I could not find any evidence that Timothy had divorced me. Our marriage was still legally binding.

My mom called the Ames, Iowa police department.

I researched bigamy and discovered that it was a class E felony in Iowa. This news brought a smile to my face; this was not a minor slip-up on his part.

My mom obtained the name and number of the officer assigned to our case – Ben of the Ames Police Department. He was immediately added to the rapidly expanding "heroes" list.

I located the address of the local police station. We were not sure if we needed to file a police report in Georgia.

My mom talked to Officer Ben; I was to submit a police report to the Ames, Iowa police department by morning.

As business hours drew to a close, we drove to the local police department. It was a dead end; the charges would have to be filed in Iowa, where the crime occurred.

We now had a course of action set out for us. We were focused and driven with one goal on our minds: have Timothy arrested and charged with felony bigamy.

Returning home, I composed and e-mailed the following to the Iowa officer:

Ben-

I received a text message from my husband, Timothy, on 7/11/09 while I was in Seattle visiting my father. The text stated that he was leaving me and leaving the state. Until this time, we had been living together as husband and wife in Lawrenceville, GA since April of 2000 (we were married in December of 1999; the marriage license is included). I have not heard from him since, despite repeated attempts to locate him.

I returned to the marital home on the morning of 7/12/09 and found the "Dear John" letter included below. On the morning of 7/13/09, I discovered that he had depleted our joint accounts and had amassed at least $150,000 in debt. He took all of the financial records with him.

On 7/16/09, I logged into his e-mail account from my computer using the password that he had given me years before. I intercepted two e-mails of note (both included). The first, sent by Amanda on 7/20/09, revealed that they were in the process of applying for visas to go to Uganda. The second, sent by Amanda on 7/24/09, revealed that Timothy and Amanda married in Ames, IA on 7/17/09. As far as I know, Timothy and I are still legally married. A records search has not turned up any divorce proceedings of which I was unaware. I secured a divorce attorney last week after receiving his "Dear John" letter, but the papers have not even been filed. A call to the records department in Iowa (where the wedding occurred) revealed that the marriage license was taken out on 7/7/09 and returned on 7/24/09, indicating that a "legal" marriage did occur.

In looking through financial documents, it is evident that my husband has been engaged in cruel deception for a number of years. The financial deceit does not appear to be illegal, just despicable, although further evidence may come to light that reveals illegal activity. From what I have found out, bigamy, which he appears to have committed on 7/17/09, is a felony. He may also be guilty of fraud (signing the marriage license stating that he was not married and evidence of continued financial deceit in the second e-mail, entitled re - wedding gig).

I would like to have him charged and prosecuted to the furthest extent of the law.
He has taken everything from me – my marriage (we had 16 I thought wonderful years together), my home, my dogs, my financial security, my trust - and I do not want him to victimize me any further. I was unaware of the

deceit and the existence of another woman until the morning of 7/13/09.

I also contacted the Gwinnett County (my county of residence) Police Department. They stated that the charges would need to be filed in Iowa, since that is where the illegal activity occurred.

Timing is critical, as it appears that they are preparing to leave for Uganda soon (next few weeks?). I know that they are currently residing in the Ames, IA area due to activity on the joint checking account (PDF of last 30 days activity included), and I would suspect that they are at her residence.

The following is the contact information that I have for Timothy and Amanda.

I included over two pages of identifying information, phone numbers, e-mails, and addresses for Timothy and Amanda using prior knowledge and what I had been able to find online.

Action dominated. The reality of the bigamy had not yet taken hold. I now had a singular focus – I wanted Timothy arrested, charged, and prosecuted for the crime, a small victory in the war that he had waged against me.

Friday ended with an e-mail to update the family.

Drumroll please...

Timothy got married in Iowa on 7/17/09.

Yes, married.

Yes, he and I are still legally married.

Yes, that is bigamy and is illegal (a felony, nonetheless).

Yes, I have filed a police report.

Forget the care package for Uganda...it looks as though the "care package" may need to go to prison.

And I just thought that no new big info had yet to be uncovered...

I forgot to mention the piñata to them. I bet they're sorry they missed it.

After sending the e-mail, I leaned back in my chair and surveyed the notes and pages of information amassed over the previous two weeks that were scattered around my computer. One date stood out: Timothy and Amanda married as I met with the bankruptcy attorney. Somehow that seemed fitting; he drained one wife in order to marry the next.

The weekend passed in a blur. The police brought Amanda and Timothy in for questioning Saturday morning. Ben quickly ascertained that Amanda was ignorant of the bigamy; she had been told that Timothy and I divorced in 2005 and he checked the box indicating "divorced" on his new marriage license. The officer called me with the updates of the questioning. Timothy was assailing him with outrageous lies. According to Timothy, he and I divorced four years ago in Gwinnett County. I had since remarried a man, Mark (or maybe it's Marc?) Mercer, and was living in Grayson, about twenty minutes from Lawrenceville. Mark (Marc?) worked as a chiropractor. We had three dogs (I wonder if these were the same ones?) and Timothy came over on occasion for dinner, as we were still friends. I guess I should be happy that if he was going to invent a new life for me, at least it seemed to be a good one.

It was a surreal few hours. The officer would e-mail me with Timothy's latest claims. Then, my mom and I would frantically sort through the limited papers, pictures, and electronic files that we had, scan if needed, and send the officer any evidence that would refute Timothy's latest lie. We have been divorced since 2005? Oh, look. Here's a dated picture of the two of us at my Teacher of the Year ceremony in 2006. Oh, we weren't really divorced, but we were separated? How about these e-mails and texts where he says versions of "I love you" up until the day before he left? And, just for fun, here are statements from friends that saw us together consistently until the end. I emptied the accounts? Oh, this will be entertaining. Here are texts where he admits he was in Brazil. Debits from my card that showed I was in Lawrenceville, and bank statements that showed thousands of dollars being deducted from his card in Brazil. Oh, and do you see this purchase? The one made right after my paycheck hit? Yup, you guessed it, those would be their wedding rings.

The pile of evidence placed in the center of the conference table between Timothy and Ben grew to epic proportions. But still he lied.

Timothy claimed he had our divorce decree over at Amanda's apartment where they were staying. He was released to obtain the document and was to return to the station with the evidence later that day. I knew no such document exited, yet I was immediately forced into a defensive position. I was aware Timothy had the skill and software required to forge such a document. It was now in a race against the clock to prove to the police that Timothy and I were still married.

It turns out that this is no easy task. Luckily, Timothy confirmed that we lived in Gwinnett, so I only had to prove that a divorce did not occur in that county. My mom and I went to the clerk's office at the courthouse and explained the situation.

"Wait, you need proof that you did NOT obtain a divorce?" said the clerk behind the computer, incredulous.

"Yes," I replied, "He's claiming that we were divorced years ago and I have to prove that we weren't so that he can be charged with bigamy."

"Bigamy?" he questioned, his eyes widening in shock. "That's unusual. I'll see what I can find."

It was a reaction I would get used to over the next few weeks.

He scanned the records by my husband's name first. That proved to be a challenge, due to my husband's common name. So, we switched to my name. There were four divorces in Gwinnett county that had a partner with my name. None of the husband's names matched.

I was relieved. Although I had no knowledge of a divorce, after what I had seen, I did not put it past Timothy to file as though I had walked away and disappeared. Maybe he tried to file via carrier pigeon not realizing that they had been extinct for the last hundred years.

"Great," my mom said. "Now, how do we communicate this to the police in Iowa?"

It took some time and conversations amongst the staff in the office, but we finally had a signed affidavit faxed to Iowa that stated that Timothy and I were still married.

Timothy was pulled back into the station the next morning. Surprisingly, he had not been able to produce the alleged divorce decree. I guess he wasn't given enough time to work his Photoshop magic on this one, especially as I later discovered that Amanda was keeping him busy with interrogations of her own.

Ben turned the theoretical screws. He informed Timothy that the more he lied, the more difficult this would be. He reminded Timothy that his vehicle, currently in the station parking lot, was marital property and could be taken from him. When he finally began to come clean to the police, Timothy threw himself a pity party. He focused on his quest for happiness and his health issues, including hypertension and occasional fainting spells. On his written statement, he indicated that he had been "suffering from a loss of conscienceness." An unintended word choice that carried with it profound meaning. Perhaps he had diagnosed the source of his medical problems.

I learned from the officer that Amanda was aiding in the arrest; Ben had been funneling some of the evidence her way to help her see the truth. Amanda was engaged in her own recognizance while helping to keep Timothy calm and at her apartment. I sensed that Amanda would have trouble coming to terms with the reality of her new husband. At 8:44 p.m. on Saturday, I sent Amanda the following message via e-mail:

Stay strong.

In the midst of the legal craziness, this was the weekend set aside to move the dogs to their new homes. Max was first; we were scheduled to drop her off at Sally's, a woman who is involved with pug rescue, on Saturday evening. She had stepped up at the last minute to provide a comfortable home for Max's last couple years. The tasks of the day were a welcome diversion; the reality of giving away my first dog did not fully take hold until we picked her up from the house.

When it hit, it hit hard. Max was the first dog that was fully mine. The first dog that I had since puppyhood. She was my constant companion. I was relieved that she had a new home, but devastated that I would have to relinquish her. The tears began on the drive to Sally's and continued as I watched Max adjust to her new surroundings. She immediately took to Cleo, the family's other pug, snuffling and wagging as pugs are wont to do. I had never seen her so relaxed upon meeting another dog. It was a good sign, but it did not hold back the tears. I sat on the floor with her for over an hour summoning up the courage to leave.

The tears continued as I walked out the door.

Glottis was slated to move to her new home on Sunday. Parents of one of my coworkers were going to keep her on their farm in Alabama. We planned to meet at the welcome center on the state line at 2:00 p.m. Glottis slept through most of the drive keeping a low profile. My mind was so occupied with other thoughts that I was able to refute the reality of what was to come. My only reminders of the imminence of the event were the mile markers counting down to Alabama.

As soon as the car slowed, Glottis began to get nervous. She had always been a very sensitive dog and was in tune with my emotions. My unease transferred to her and she began to chuff at everyone around her. As her new owners had not yet arrived, I decided to take Glottis on a run around the wooded area surrounding the welcome center. As long as she was running, she was calm. Like mother, like daughter. We sweated out some of our anxiety together.

Glottis's new caretaker pulled into the parking lot and approached us as we sat at a concrete picnic table. Glottis barked, hiding behind my legs, unsure of the newcomer. My tears began to flow again. Her new momma was wonderfully patient, ignoring the fearful dog for several minutes while engaging in light conversation. Glottis slowly started to relax; I could feel her muscles loosen where she was pressed against me. I slid a bag of dog cookies over to her new owner. She slowly took one and held it out to Glottis. It was accepted, but immediately expelled onto the ground. Too soon.

Time passed. Glottis tentatively nosed the cookie on the ground, and finally cautiously consumed it. Another cookie was offered. This one was accepted without reservation. The transfer of loyalty had begun. As we continued to talk, Glottis slowly inched her way closer to the giver of the treats. I tried to choke back my tears as I handed the leash over. I sealed the deal by placing Glottis's belongings in her car and walking away, leaving my youngest behind.

Another shard of my shattered life retrieved by another. I could only hope that enough fragments of my previous existence would remain in my possession to build a cohesive mosaic of a life again.

I received news on Monday morning that Timothy had been arrested. His car (legally, *our* car), a 2005 Toyota 4Runner, had been placed in an impound lot that was difficult to find. The officer suggested that my mom and I make a trip to Iowa, complete the paperwork associated with the case, and bring the car back to Atlanta. I never would have thought of that idea, but there was certainly an appeal to leaving him stranded with nothing. A little attorney-approved tit for tat.

I felt a strange nervous excitement knowing he was behind bars. I had to smile, thinking of him alongside harder criminals. I hoped he had learned something from the prison documentaries we sometimes watched. I hoped he was scared. I hoped he felt alone. I hoped he had time to think about what he had done. I hoped his cellmate was named, "Bubba."

My mom and I had an hour before we had to go to the divorce attorney's office for an appointment. We stopped at a Wendy's so that Mom could get some lunch and we could both get some phone calls made. As it became clear that we were moving forward with the vehicle retrieval trip to Iowa, we began to put things into motion so that we could leave early the next morning. My mom began calling her clients and canceling the phone appointments scheduled for the next two days. I called my dad and set him loose on the task of finding plane tickets. I contacted Ben to let him know that the trip was a go.

In between these calls, my mom and I made plans, notes, and predictions. Our conversations with each other casually included the words bigamy, prison, bond, and probation. Our reality had shifted, these words no longer felt foreign on our lips. At one point, my focus lapsed and I glanced around the dining room to see a dozen people, dressed smartly in business casual, staring at us. Oh yeah, I guess this isn't quite normal. Bigamy isn't part of the lunchtime crowd's lexicon. Welcome to my afternoon soap opera now served alongside your Frosty for your lunchtime entertainment.

While in the lobby of the attorney's office, I received a call from Timothy's boss, the one who had dismissed me when I called him two weeks prior.

He barked, "Where is he?"

"He's in jail. I was told that his computers have been compounded; I don't know if they are the business ones. There may be evidence on them," I informed him with not a little smugness. "Oh," I added, "You may also want to know that he and his wife were about to leave for Uganda."

"What? He has a project due tomorrow!" his boss replied, alarm entering into voice.

"Well, I guess you better try to find someone else who can do it. Good luck with that. Bye, now." I felt no sympathy for the man whom I discovered had helped Timothy lie about the affair and the trip to Brazil. He could now deal with the consequences of supporting deception.

"So, I guess this changes things," said the divorce attorney as we entered her office. We had been keeping her apprised of the bigamy proceedings. We quickly drafted up new papers: a fault divorce that we prepared to serve to him while he was in jail. It turns out that there was no legal code that could be found for bigamy, so we settled on infidelity. While we working on the papers, the officer e-mailed Timothy's mug shot to us.

Cold, dead eyes stared back at me. I closely examined the picture, scanning his face for any signs of the man I had loved two weeks prior. He was not there; he had been completely swallowed by a shadow that darkened his features and hardened his gaze.

By the time we left the attorney's office, we had the prepared divorce documents to serve him and, thanks to my dad, we had plane tickets for the next morning to Des Moines, Iowa where we would take a shuttle to Ames. The ride of the last two weeks had certainly accelerated.

Monday night brought with it the appointment to relinquish the final dog. I'm not sure if it was due to my emotional reservoir running dry or Porter being primarily Timothy's dog, but I was not as tearful at the thought of this parting. Porter's new owner, Brenda, was a fellow teacher who had just finalized an ugly divorce. She needed a friend, a protector. Porter needed the same. They would be a perfect match.

Brenda's biggest concern was that Porter wouldn't like her; my biggest worry was that she wouldn't accept Porter. Neither of us had anything to worry about. He greeted her warmly and quickly took to his new surroundings, testing the pushability of the open French door with his nose and rubbing the rug lovingly with his back. He had found a home.

No tears fell as we left Brenda's. They remained absent for the next several weeks, anxiety and anger replacing the sadness.

In the midst of moving the dogs and defending my marital status, I had maintained some contact with Amanda. I re-sent her the two e-mails that I intended for Timothy as she had only received one of them.

I wish this had gotten through to me on Wednesday.

My God, what have I done...I do hope you know that we are both victims in this (I think you do), and that it looks certain that they will arrest him on Monday, and it will all come out. I don't know how you or I can ever feel safe again, let alone trust anyone.

This is sickening. I have never imagined anyone could do this.

He must be a sociopath...

I am so sorry, Lisa.

Amanda

I gave her his birth date so that she could continue her own sleuthing.

I returned home from Brenda's on Monday to find the following message.

Hi Lisa,

I am sure you know how things have progressed here.

Timothy is in jail and the police have his computers, and the car is in their parking lot until you order private towing.

I wanted to ask you if you wanted to look through the rest of his things before either I donate them or he tells the officer that he wants them back (if he bonds himself out of jail). I am in this apartment until Thursday or Friday, when my lease ends, and his stuff will be here until then, unless he comes with the officer to claim it.

His bicycle is here as well. I don't know if it is worth anything, but you might want to take it.

Just let me know.

I am in shock right now, though not as much as you have to be.

Please call me if you have any questions or want to meet when you get here. I teach until 1230pm Tuesday through Thursday, but otherwise am wide open for you when you get here.

I am here for you.

Amanda

Strangely excited to talk to my husband's wife, I picked up the phone.

Amanda and I talked for 2 ½ hours. Fact checking. Questioning. Filling in the gaps. Putting together pieces. It was strange to finally be getting some answers. Stranger still, to be getting them from her. She had gone from a faceless entity, to a known rival, to an ally, all in the span of a week.

It was immediately clear that Timothy had fabricated an entire false persona and existence that he portrayed to Amanda. They met in Las Vegas in March when they were both there on business. They spent time together during that trip, confirming that his boss did know about the affair. They maintained contact over the next few months. He visited Iowa every few weeks and they had two weeks in Brazil together. That was it. They married three months after meeting. She had never met any of his friends or family.

She was not the woman who had been in the house. She was not with him on the dinners out I found on the accounts that were too expensive for one person. Who was?

His stories to her knew no limits.

He claimed to be one-third owner of GS, a company that he had worked along side of for years. He used that assertion to run up Amanda's credit cards; he led her to believe that he would be receiving a great deal of money soon for selling his share. The only company he ever owned was MMS, a now defunct LLC that operated out of his office for a year. It wasn't even worth the cost of the paper the business license was printed upon.

In his stories to Amanda, a friend, who works as a graphic designer, became the realtor, selling Timothy's house in Atlanta. I had apparently already moved out to live with Mythical Mark Mercer several years earlier. The designer cum realtor was holding an open house the weekend of the wedding and reputedly a nice military couple was interested in the property. I wished this couple existed; it would be nice to be able to avoid foreclosure.

He told her that he and I maintained a friendship and that I frequently watched his dog, Porter, for him. That was nice of him to keep one of his dogs in his story. Amanda demanded to view some of the friendly e-mails between Timothy and I that he claimed proved our ongoing *friend*ship. Desperate, Timothy logged in to my e-mail account (ahh, *that's* why I was kicked out) and sent some e-mails from "me" to him. Amusingly, they were all dated July 26, 2009 and included the message, "Merry Christmas." Oops. I guess his desperation finally let some errors slip through.

Most disturbingly, Amanda related that she discovered that he was in the process of taking out a life insurance policy on her. She also found pages where he was practicing her signature.

"Thank you for figuring this out. I don't think I would have made it out of Uganda alive," she stated in an alarmed voice.

We both were in shock. We both had trusted this man. I was trying to reconcile 16 years with him with this current knowledge; she was trying to handle the fact that she married a falsehood outright. We both felt angry, confused, betrayed, and conned. We bonded in our victimhood. We felt like wives of Henry VIII, used and discarded in an ever-expanding quest for power. Thankfully, we both still had our heads.

All his lies had an element of truth, a kernel that helped to solidify the falsehood, like the dust that seeds a cloud. He was clever; he only told lies that were difficult to disprove. He was cunning; he had different stories for different people. He was crafty; telling people what they wanted to hear. He was depraved; he acted as a puppet master with no thoughts for those anchored unknowingly to his strings.

Since receiving the e-mail that disclosed the bigamy, I had alternated between tears and laughter. The former precipitated by the dogs and the latter erupted from the sheer absurdity of the soap opera that was impersonating my life. I walked a tightrope between sorrow and a perverse glee as he faced his first consequences. Laughter and tears are both born of strong emotion and they are only separated by a thin veil.

That night was characterized by jokes about bigamy. I pondered what Ms. Manners would say if she knew I was not invited to the wedding. We thought about writing an advice column, "If you're going to get married illegally, be sure to pay the band." I wondered how I should refer to Amanda; is she my wife-in-law? "My husband's wife" was becoming confusing and a bit clumsy and "sister wife" implied our consent to the arrangement. The laughter belied our anxiety and sadness; it was a desperate tool to keep the demons at bay, even if just for the night.

My mom and I awoke to our alarm clocks at 3:00 a.m. Tuesday morning after a restless night. We stumbled to her rental car and made the drive to the Atlanta airport, not sure what we were heading towards.

"Dear John" Letter Fourth Interpretation (July 24, 2009)

Lisa,

I'm afraid there is no easy way for me to say this – I'm leaving. *Leaving sanity, for sure.* We have had a long and rich life together but I can no longer live this life anymore. *You forgot one important thing – generally a divorce is filed before one participates in a second wedding.* As I told you several months ago, I feel as though we have been drifting apart for a number of years. *Funny. You met Amanda several months ago.* It was a gradual thing but I can honestly say that it has reached a point where I no longer can share time with you without wondering when I can be away from you again. *You are certainly "away" now.* I can't keep living this lie – it's not fair to either one of us. *You do realize that your entire new life is based on a lie? Bigamy IS a form of fraud.* I will continue to support you as best I can from wherever I end up. *Amanda's marital bed?* I will continue to work for DS but I would appreciate if you didn't involve them in this matter. *Aren't they going to wonder how a marriage occurred so quickly?* We had some amazing times together and I will treasure these memories for the rest of my life. *How can you? You will never be able to speak of me to your wife?* I think people change as they experience life and unfortunately we have grown so far apart that I simply cannot relate to you in any way. **You changed into a felon.** I know that this will hit you very hard and for that I am sincerely sorry. **Not as hard as prison will hit you and for that I am NOT sincerely sorry.** I have never wanted to do anything to harm you in any way but in doing so I have made myself unhappy for many years. **You certainly have an interesting way of seeking happiness.** I know that once you recover from the shock of this you will bounce back and live a happy and satisfying life – a better and more honest life than I could ever hope to offer you. **When will the shocks stop?** Everything I have left behind is yours and all I have taken is my clothing and the equipment I need to make a living. **...and the birth certificate you needed for your marriage license.** I will never ask you for forgiveness or understanding. **I hope you don't expect these from the courts, either.**

I am a coward who couldn't tell you to your face that I am leaving. **Or tell me that you were getting married. You are sick.** If I don't do this now then I probably never will. **Knowing what I know now, I wish you hadn't taken so long to leave.** I need my life to have some sort of meaning to it and unfortunately working in the basement of my house and watching tv and playing video games isn't it. **I hope that you find prison meaningful.**

I'm sorry but my life is very quickly becoming that of my parents. **Their life is pretty plain Jane vanilla next to** *what you've concocted.* No matter how much I see that, it feels like there is nothing I can do to change the path that I am on. *Why? Because the wedding deposits are nonrefundable?* From this point on there is nothing more that I can say other than how sorry I am for leaving you in this way. *...and you didn't even send me a wedding invitation. I'm sure Emily Post would agree that that was rude.* I will do everything I can from this point forward to try and make this as easy on you as possible. *What will your wife think of that?* I didn't strip the account to leave. *Nope, just stripped it to woo Amanda.* I sold everything downstairs that I felt was part of the old me that I so desperately need to leave behind. *You certainly left the old you behind. I wonder how much of the old you Amanda is even aware of?*

Lesson Five

There is No Shame in Asking For Help

I have always been very independent. As a very young (and short) child, I would use household objects as tools in order to reach the light switches so that I would not have to depend upon anyone else. This trait did not have an inverse relationship with my height; if anything, I became more wilful as I grew up. My stubborn independence was a point of contention in my marriage.

"Damn it, Lisa. Just let me help," was a common refrain with me only giving in once I tired of his bull-like insistence. In my mind, needing help was a sign of weakness, an indicator of ineptitude. I felt like I needed to prove, even to him, that I could do it alone.

He eventually took me up on that challenge, and, as a result, put me a position where I had to accept help just to survive. Crisis has a knack for washing away pride just as cleanly as the Greek gods struck down anyone possessed with hubris in a single lightening bolt.

My husband had delivered a package of explosives with that text. Detonation was inevitable; it was too late to call in the bomb squad. Luckily, it was not too late for a balm squad to assemble: family and friends willing and able to offer support.

The e-mails of support from family began to arrive almost immediately. The first outside my parents came from my aunt, who lives with her husband in Wisconsin.

July 13, 2009

Lisa,

Life sure sucks sometimes! We are truly sorry for all you are going through.....and stunned to say the least. So glad your dad has been able to be with you at this time. With so many logistics to work out at this point, I am sure he is of great assistance to help you begin to pick up the pieces. One thing is an absolute, Lisa. You are a brilliant, talented, strong, beautiful young woman who we have NO doubt will come out the other side of this horrible mess in one piece, stronger than you ever imagined you could be. I know you don't feel that way now......and you have a lot of steps to walk before you will begin to see the light again.....but just keep on putting one foot in front of the other, and you WILL get there!

I know you haven't begun to know what you want to do yet, but I wanted to be sure that you know our home is your home. If you should decide you need to relocate somewhere that does not have unbearable summers and are looking for a place *near family with a <u>great variety of seasons</u>, our home is open to you for as long as you need. We have actually had a picture perfect couple of weeks! And Ariana and Julia were quick to say "she should come here!" Now that Ariana will be gone most of the time, it should even be quiet......although Julia is moving this week to an apartment a mile or so down the road from us, so she is sure to drop in often!!*

James has spoken with Olivia regarding possible jobs in Wisconsin, and she will be sending you a web site to peruse. I'm sure Olivia would be a great educator resource for you here, if this is even a possibility for you. Keep it in mind. We love you and would love to help you get back on your feet.

Love,
Sue

I could feel a little strength returning. This was quickly followed by a message from my cousin's wife, whom I had only met once.

Hello Lisa,

I can't begin to express how my heart goes out to you. If there is anything William and I can do, don't hesitate to ask – anything at all.

There is a website where (almost) all the teaching jobs are advertised/posted. It lacks a few private schools in the area, but for the most part it is inclusive. I have heard that Madison tends to post/hire late in the summer and at the start of the year so there might be opportunities coming available.

I also am including the department of public instruction licensing page. If you are licensed in another state and went through a state approved certification program you should be able to get a Wisconsin license with a relatively small amount of hoop jumping (you know how it goes!). If there are any questions you have please know that you can call (or e-mail) anytime.

Take care, and again, anything we can do.

~Olivia (and William)

I could not do this alone. I was so lucky that I did not have to try. The next message was from Grace, a long-time family friend based in San Antonio. It was sent to my new e-mail address, which included the words July Dis*ss*ter. The two s's were important.

7/16 Grace

you go girl!! is next month's e-address going to be something like Lisa <kickbuttaugust@...> ?!

i know that, in addition to your own perseverance and ability to get up & go, you've got a great team of friends & family on your side. i know from my own experience, what an incredible powerhouse and there for you support your mom can be. will be interesting to see what phoenix rises from these ashes....

all the best,

Grace

P.S. y'know if you end up hanging around Alamo City, there's room in my inn ... it's even furnished!

This was followed by a message from my step-sister, Lauren, and her wife who live in Oregon.

7/16 Lauren & Anna

Dear Lisa,

I just heard about what happened, and I am so sorry. Timothy is such an unbelievable jerk! I can't think of a strong enough word for his behavior. Actually, I can think of a lot of words, but none of them quite capture it, even strung together at high volume, with explanatory gestures.

I don't mean to sound "shrinky" but... just in case you are feeling like this is somehow your fault or you should have done something to prevent it—remember that there is absolutely nothing you could ever have done to deserve something like this. No one deserves to be treated the way he treated you. And there is nothing you could have done to prevent it; this is

119

clearly something he has been planning for a long time and nothing you said or did would have made a difference. It is about him and whatever his issues are, not you.

I am so glad that you have a good support network, that your mom and dad and friends are there for you, and that you have a good lawyer. I know your mom is incredibly proud of how you've handled the situation. It will be very up and down for a long time, but you will survive this and thrive. I have always thought you were driven, creative, confident, and clear-headed, and I know that will help you get through this terrible time.

Please let me know if there is anything I can do for you, and I'll be thinking of you.

Lauren

Of course, I am also thinking of you. Your situation is worse than a bad oxygen-channel movie, and I can't imagine what you must have felt learning one horrible thing after another after another. I can only tell you that even though we have not known each other very well, I hold you in the space reserved for family in my heart. I know it is unlikely I can do anything for you, and you shouldn't call for my sake, or because I offered, if there does happen to be anything I can do, don't hesitate to let me know. I will be happy to be there for you.

With sympathy from your sister-out-law,

Anna

Next came a message from a stepbrother in Austin. It was a good thing I played *Where in the World is Carmen Santiago* as a kid; my geography was certainly being put to the test.

7/16 Mike

Hey Lisa,

We just heard from Cathy this afternoon about the totally horrible stuff going on this week. I'm really heartbroken for you - this sounds like a totally unbearable thing to have dropped in your lap. It's also totally shocking, since Timothy always seemed really engaged and loving (at least in the small time I've been able to spend with y'all). The whole thing leaves me (and probably you) at somewhat of a loss - it's just hard to comprehend.

Anyway, I really just wanted to let you know that I'm sending you good thoughts and hoping that you're doing ok. I'm also at your disposal for anything I could possibly do to help, whatever that might be. If you don't already, you should know that you have lots of people in your corner.

Also, I'm sure you have a lot going on already, so it's up to you whether or when to write back - whatever works best.

Take care,

Mike

I was overwhelmed at the thought of trying to craft individual responses at that point, so I crafted a single response to send to the entire group.

July 19, 2009   8:41 p.m.

Thank you for your thoughts - I would not be able to make it right now without the support of those around me. I'm sending one message to everyone, because I don't think I can compose multiple responses.

Obviously, I am absolutely shattered and shocked by this. I discovered that what I cherished most in life was a cruel lie. I am in the very early stages of rebuilding (or actually building, since I have never been an adult without Timothy) a life. An amazing friend has opened her home to me and it is an amazing environment to help me heal. My immediate plans are to stay in the Atlanta area for the upcoming school year and most likely relocate next summer (Atlanta has too many memories). I am not sure yet where I will land. I have to place my beloved dogs with new owners because I am not able to care for them at this point. I am facing bankruptcy due to his financial deceptions and I am obviously filing for divorce as soon as possible. The process will be long, partly because he is not reachable (not that I want any contact at this point).

I know that many of us are trying to reconcile the Timothy we knew with what we now know. I don't believe that we will ever understand his thinking. I am trying to avoid spending too much time unraveling his many deceptions and trying to find meaning in his actions. I need to focus on me and on the future. He has taken everything away from me but I won't let him have the rest of my life. I am hopeful that I can get to a point where I can remember some of the times I had with him with fondness. Sixteen years is a lot to lose. I am at peace with my part of this; I know that I did nothing to cause him to act this way and that I could not have changed the outcome even if I had received any advanced notice. I hope that in the future I will be able to find an honest version of the marriage that I had.

I am so lucky to have the family I do. If it wasn't for my dad, I would still be on the floor at my aunt and uncle's house in Eugene. He dropped everything to get me back to Atlanta and he got me through this first week of hell. My mom comes out today (which is good, because I think I've exhausted my dad at this point) to work on the next steps and to help me get ready for the school year. Thanks to the financial support of my parents and my uncle David, I have the money needed to secure attorneys and to start to rebuild.

I know that everybody wants to help, but is not quite sure how. Here are a few ideas:

-Please don't talk to me about trying to figure out the whys/whats/hows...I am having a hard enough time trying to avoid them on my own and they don't help me move on.

-At some point, I may want to talk about positive memories of him.

-I always appreciate gallows humor.

-I am working on a revenge fantasy list - feel free to contribute (no censorship needed).

-I will most likely relocate near family. I also need to consider work opportunities and the "feel" of the place. Please don't take it personally if I don't choose your area.

-I'm not quite the same Lisa right now. I'm angry and very emotional. Please be patient and help me learn to trust again.

-The best thing anyone can do for me right now is initiate/maintain contact. As you all know, I pretty much suck at that and I don't need to be isolated right now.

Again, thank all of you for you thoughts and support. I truly could not do this without all of you.

The responses started arriving almost immediately.

7/18/09

I absolutely love that you gave us a list of tips! That is really helpful and I will try to follow them starting with… contact! But don't feel you need to get back with me immediately or at all, I

124

know you are incredibly busy right now.

With the relocation, if Portland is on your list, I have a guest room with your name on it if you want to visit and check it out. However, the economy sucks, the unemployment rate is high, and housing is expensive. It's also really awesome and I love it here. I can get you in e-mail contact with several local teacher friends if you are interested.

With the revenge fantasy list... hmmm. I'm thinking public humiliation followed by banishment...

First (this isn't the revenge part yet), all the debts he took out which affect you will be erased, your credit score will be increased to one million, and you will win the lottery, the proceeds of which you will use to set up a generous annuity and to buy a flying castle (staffed with oiled, manly servants who are of course compensated with a living wage, health insurance, dental, and vision) so you can relocate wherever you want with all your animals.

Then, Timothy will take a world tour (nude, with a powerful air-conditioner pointed at him at all times) in a cage labeled "I am Timothy, the world's biggest asshole. Please read on to learn about my crimes and myriad inadequacies, which are detailed below." Crowds of millions will greet him at every stop, throwing rotten fruit and vegetables, poking him with sticks, making rude gestures, and calling him inventive names in every language under the sun (he will be accompanied at all times by a translator so he won't miss a thing, and the translator will smell really, really bad). All the people in the crowd will hold up signs saying things like "Timothy, you incredible asshat" and "Lisa is the awesomest." After the world tour, when he is thoroughly humiliated and demoralized, he will be banished for life, without a hat or sunscreen, to a desert island. There will be nothing to eat but moldy bread and nothing to drink but warm flat Pepsi that has a funny smell, and his only companions will be people exactly like him and giant bird-eating spiders, which will get increasingly frustrated and hungry since there will be no birds. And it will get worse from there.

Sending you good thoughts,

Lauren

I love my family. Lauren's dad, my stepfather, followed:

Lisa -

Thanks so much for including me in the letter. I want to support you in any way possible. Please don't take my silence as disinterest. I went looking for a card to send you, but didn't find any appropriate "Hope you get revenge" messages. I did not think that calling to talk would help at all. Know that you are in my thoughts.

When this began Cathy was afraid for you and I just listened, but inside I had no doubt that you had the strength, fortitude and drive to get through this successfully. Yes, another damn growth experience. A huge one.

I figure that my best help right now is to keep our home front going so your mom can concentrate on the tasks at hand and not worry about life and home in San Antonio.

My revenge fantasy is that Bimbo is really a smarter con artist than Timothy and will take him for a financial downfall ride that he will regret for years to come. :-)

I guess you heard my mom's: A continuous blow torch to the toes.

Call me any time.

Love,
John

7/19/09

Thanks for the info, and for the ideas on how to help out. I wanted to ask how I could help, but didn't want to add yet another thing to your list.

I like the idea of the revenge fantasy list (and hopefully I'm understanding the intended spirit of such), so I suggest we form a Special Committee of Revenge for Egregious Wrongdoing To a Bride, which conveniently abbreviates as SCREW T.B. (of course I don't actually imagine there will be a real committee, but the name is the important part)

Given my computer-y leanings, I think a great revenge idea would be to write a computer virus (I suggest Tourette.Win32.B as the official designation) that would infect his e-mail server and replace random words in his outgoing mail with all-caps vulgarities, and add an appropriate nickname to his name in the sender field (e.g. Timothy "Asshole" Black). I will work on other ideas as well.

I also offer this amusing cat picture in hopes of putting a smile on your face.

Well I hope there might be a chance for you and Cathy to do something enjoyable while she's there, but regardless, I'm glad to know that she's there with you. It's also good to hear that your dad has been such a great source of strength/aid through this; that sounds like a wonderful thing.

That's all I've got for the moment; responses are enjoyed but not required, and I'll be in touch again soon.

Take care,
Mike

Hi Lisa,

Mike and I came up with a suggestion for revenge and gallows humor fun… how about a contest to come up with the best acronym for T.I.M.O.T.H.Y.? The winner would get eternal glory and bragging rights. People could enter as often as they want (with no purchase necessary). Here are some options to start things off:

The Impotent Mean Ogre-like Tactless Hateful Yo-yo

Tragically Ignorant Mendacious Outrageously Tapewormed and Horrible Yahoo

Tell us what you think, and we are thinking of you.

Lauren, Mike, and Anna

Once I had found out about Amanda and the upcoming trip to Uganda, I sent the following to update the family:

Intercepted an e-mail this morning that revealed the following information:

-his honey (I now have her name/picture) is a PhD candidate at University of Iowa in Geography

-he is applying for a visa (that should be amusing)

-and the BIG one, they are going to Uganda soon (I have his contact number there) I guess he really is running.

And the funny, here is the tag line on her e-mail:

> > Don't wait for strangers to remind you of your duty,

> > you have a conscience and a spirit for that.

> > All the good you do must come from your own initiative.

> > -Popul Vuh

Of, course, the family couldn't stay silent after that bombshell.

Wow, that's even weirder. At any rate, we'll have to factor Uganda into the revenge fantasies. I don't know if you saw Slumdog Millionaire, but I'm thinking of something like the outhouse escape scene, with a much bigger and deeper shit pond. They probably have some outhouses in Uganda, right?

Also, in reference to your previous e-mail, it would be kickass if you ended up relocating to central Texas, but as you say, I won't be in the least offended if you don't. I'm sure that decision is a long way off anyway.

- Mike

Who gets a PhD in Geography? What is she going to do, make really expensive maps? Teach people to make maps? That is so dumb.

Does he owe the feds any money? If so, he may not have a valid passport. That would be pretty funny.

Do you already have a flag on your credit report? I think there is something you can do to say someone has been using your credit without your permission (but it might only be for identity theft?). Protection for you and a nice surprise for him.

That tag line is hilarious.

Love, Lauren

Okay sibs (and Anna), it is ON! T.I.M.O.T.H.Y., the fun game of mean-spirited acronyms with the fabulous prize of bragging rights, starts now. Mike, do you think your wife wants to play?

Here is my entry for today:

Toad-faced Iguana-breathed Mosquito-brained Onager-assed Tick-covered Hog-smelling Yak

Can I get a round of applause for the animal theme?

Lauren

I believe my wife is going to opt out on the grounds of extreme grad-student brain-fry, but I'm in.

Today's submission: Treasonous Ignoramus Miserable Offering Terrible Half-wit Yap

Also, I love the animal theme (insert clapping here).

love,
Mike

How about...

Treacherous Inconsiderate Miscreant-y Opportunistic Thieving Hypocritical Yeast-head

See Mike's masterpiece below.

Lauren

And today's rather linguistically-challenged entry:

Turpitudinous Infectious Moronic Oafish Travesty-of-a-man Hooligan Moronic Trenchfooted Yahoo

"Turpitude" is a noun, but it was too appropriate to pass up, so I improvised.

- Mike

My e-mails to the family were not as humorous as theirs to me, but I felt like I needed to keep them informed. I sent another e-mail to make sure everyone was following the twists and turns of the rapidly unfolding events.

7/23/09

Here's the latest:

-I intercepted an e-mail that contained lots of valuable info and easily led to more info

-girlfriend's name, job, phone numbers, e-mail addresses, home address (in Iowa, where they currently are), and some personal info from blogs, etc.

-the fact that they are planning to go to Uganda soon (couple of weeks?)

-contact info in Uganda

-I sent him a pretty powerful e-mail yesterday through her (I don't have his new e-mail) & I followed up with copies sent to his place of work, her home, and her work (all addressed to him). It brought me some peace to be able to say the stuff I needed to say. I also hope that it brings some fear, guilt, and pain to him by my holding a mirror up to what he has done and showing him the devastation that he has caused and tried to run away from.

-The legal stuff is in motion, but moving slowly. For the purpose of the legal stuff, it is best if he stays "missing," which doesn't seem to be a problem. I hope to be divorced and bankrupt by Christmas. That's a sentence I never imagined writing.

-The two younger dogs are going to separate homes on Sunday. Both homes seem like a good match. Max, the elder pug, still does not have a home. I'm going to try to keep the kitty.

-I'm trying to gear up for the start of the school year on August 3. I have to say that it is hard to focus too much on work right now.

-My current plans are to stay in Atlanta through the end of the school year& then move to the greater Seattle area next summer. I'm in the VERY early stages of job hunting there.

-The people around me have continued to be amazing. I could not do this alone. Please keep sending the humor & revenge fantasies...they help keep me going. My latest revenge idea - I would love to have a "care package" waiting for him in Uganda that of course would have to contain pictures of his "loving family" back home. Couldn't you just see the look of shock on his face when he realized that I reached him in Africa?

-He actually only locked me out of receiving my e-mail...I can still send MMS messages and I still get at least some of his e-mail.

-The dumbass is still sending his paychecks to the joint account. I left $1.32 in checking and moved the rest to savings with no overdraft protection. Wouldn't that be a lovely place to get $ for a donation for Max?

I'm certainly having better days (can't quite call them "good" yet) and bad days. I'm continuing to try to focus on the future and not spend too much time or energy unraveling the past.

Love to you all,

Lisa

Apart from my family spread around the country, I was also receiving amazing support in Atlanta. Coworkers called to check on me and offered to help when I stopped by the school. A few spearheaded the hunt for homes for the dogs. Several offered me a place to stay, addressing one of the most critical needs I faced at the time: low-cost housing in an understanding and supportive environment.

The Ronald McDonald House is an organization that provides free or low-cost housing for families who have a child undergoing treatment in a hospital in a city away from their hometown. The homes are designed to be welcoming and comfortable and provide a haven for the family while they are dealing with stress and uncertainty.

I think that same model could work for the recently separated.

When my husband disappeared, I found myself with a home I could not afford (literally or emotionally), no family in the city where I was employed, and I knew that I should not live alone (not that I was in any shape to go apartment hunting). I was fortunate. Very fortunate.

My friends Sarah and Curtis were ready and willing to offer shelter. Sanctuary. My living space went from 2500 square feet to 250, as I made my bed using borrowed sheets on a guest bed under a

University of Tennessee poster. I downsized from a full kitchen to a few shelves in the breakfast nook. My custom-built office, lovingly crafted by Timothy, was replaced by a folding card table against one wall in the upstairs bonus room. It was perfect.

Sarah and I had met years earlier when we were both teaching eighth grade at the same school. We hit it off immediately and had become close friends. She and her husband had settled in a suburban community not far from me, as they began to temper their earlier lifestyles in preparation for adopting a baby. The long-anticipated adoption occurred in the spring of 2009, when they became the proud parents of Kayla, a beautiful little girl who was going through her own challenges. Kalya was born at 32 weeks and had gastroschisis, which necessitated surgery when she was just a few days old. For weeks, Sarah and Curtis spent every available moment at the hospital where the staff worked to help tiny Kayla gain the weight she needed in order to go home. Finally, as May turned into June, she was released.

I visited the new family on her third day home. Their entire world had shrunk to the master bedroom, which contained all of the needed equipment. Kayla was tied to a feeding tube and an alarm, programmed to sound an alert anytime she stopped breathing. An alarm we grew too familiar with in those early weeks. Her frail, three-pound body was covered in fine hair that softened her eggshell skin stretched over blue veins. She looked so fragile, but she would prove to us that she was a fighter.

That home, which I stayed in for a year, was a key component of my healing. It was a safe place, filled with the sounds and energy of family. It was space where I could cry, scream, and curse (as long as it wasn't nap time). It was a house that provided normalcy as my friend and I engaged in our usual debates. It was a place for gaining strength. The baby and I were both placed on weight-gaining diets. It was a home that welcomed me as I was.

Not everyone undergoing a divorce has the opportunity to be in such a place. But maybe they should. Perhaps we could have transitional homes for those who are leaving one life behind and unsure of what the new life will entail. Homes where discussions of depositions, custody, and infidelity are just normal nighttime ramblings. Spaces where we can scream the anger out and cry the hurt out, until we are ready to leave intact, ready to face the world again.

If I had hooked myself up to Kayla's alarm system that summer, its sirens would have been screaming as it failed to detect enough breath to maintain life.

My body began to break down from the constant anxiety and the lack of sleep that accompanied it. Adding fuel to the corporeal conflagration was my lack of nutrition; my normally regimented eating habits were severely diminished. I had lost almost twenty pounds in two weeks from my already slim frame. Visible and tangible veins crossed my body, giving me a vulnerable otherworldly appearance. My body trembled constantly both from tension and from exhaustion. My mind, normally so quick and sharp, began to struggle to process even simple demands. It was clear that I needed help; my stubborn independence was not sufficient to heal my body and my mind.

I knew that I would have to give into medication; my reluctance to alter my chemistry was no longer healthy. With the help of my mom, I secured an emergency appointment with a psychiatrist. My mom sent an advance e-mail that summarized my story.

CONFIDENTIAL INFORMATION

I am attempting to assist my daughter, Lisa Arends, at a time of trauma, where she needs support. She gave me permission to write to you, saying she just didn't have the energy to do this right now. I will be returning soon to San Antonio after staying with her for two weeks. Her father, who lives in Seattle, is also part of her support team and spent the first week with her, after the trauma that started 7/11/09, has left Lisa without sleeping and eating, of which we are both seriously concerned.

BEFORE:

Lisa has been with her husband for 16yrs. They met when they were 15yrs old and have been together ever since, marrying in 1999. To all appearances, they looked like the ideal couple. He was loving, patient, giving, caring, attentive, etc. The kind where others would think, "Gee, I wish I had a husband like that". Very intelligent, very talented, did a zillion things around the house with projects he and Lisa did together as an incredible team. Lisa teaches at a middle school, where she was Teacher of the Year, youngest ever at the school and first year she was eligible.

SERIES OF TRAUMAS IN 3 WEEK TIME OF JULY:

*(1) * Started July 11th, with a totally unexpected text message from her husband, Timothy, "I'm leaving, moving out of state. Can't live like this anymore. Dogs are in the basement, here's the garage code."*

This was sent to Lisa while she was visiting her father in Seattle. Text messages and calls preceding this were the usual "I love you, can't wait to see you". His goodbye to her at airport when she left for the trip, "the week will go fast, we'll be back together soon."

She and her dad flew back to Atlanta on an all night flight. Got to house, to be greeted by a

(2) very cold, very cruel "Dear John" letter. Also house

(3) had signs of another female having been there.

Now starts the not sleeping, not eating of the past almost 3 weeks now. Core reason Lisa is seeking you out for your help as first need.

This turned out to be only the beginning of a continuous unfolding of more traumas over the next 2 weeks, blow after blow.

Timothy had done all the finances the last few years. Lisa loved, trusted, adored him. Had no reason not to.

After this happened, and she returned to the house, Lisa got on line to try to access the accounts. When Timothy left, he took all of their financial info and records with him since 2004. In spite of him changing access codes, passwords to accounts, Lisa managed to get in. What she discovered was horrifying for her. Checking account $200 below water. Savings account at $5.32. Then she started to see signs of huge expenditures she knew nothing about. Long story short, creditors started showing up at the door the next few days. It quickly

(4)became apparent that he had built a financial nightmare of around $160,000 of debt that was now caving in and he had run from it. This was all totally hidden from Lisa and lied about. Total deceit and manipulation on his part over and over. Lisa was left with no money at all and no access to money until the end of the month with her paycheck coming in. A new account was set up for her and family wired money in.

Lisa went into action immediately:

* contacted friend, packed her clothes, moved out to stay at spare bedroom at friends house

* divorce lawyer hired

* bankruptcy lawyer hired

saw her ob-gyn for STD testing, offered Lisa medication, but Lisa turned it down at that time, not wanting to do medication. Lisa was violently shaking with anxiety throughout that appt and with any creditor stuff. Problem was when Lisa was ready to agree to medication, a few days later, the doctor was out of town on vacation for a week. Other doctor in practice there prescribed 10 of Ambien-CR, till Lisa could get to psychiatrist. That has allowed her to sleep 3 hrs, then the anxiety pushed through it and she is awake at 3am, again unable to sleep.

Conclusion at this time, Lisa will have to:

(5) foreclose on the beautiful house she has poured her heart and soul into and

(6) file for bankruptcy to protect herself from creditors of his debt.

Meanwhile, Lisa was playing detective, watching Timothy's activity on his ATM withdrawals, when his weekly paycheck was getting deposited into their joint checking account. She could tell he was in Ames, IA. There had been several airfare charges to that location, which pointed to suspicion of girlfriend there.

The next week, Lisa found 2 e-mails a few days apart, in Timothy's junk mail account, that took the whole tragedy to a bizarre level.

(7) First intercepted e-mail indicated, yes, there is a girlfriend and they were doing their visas to leave the country for Uganda very shortly.

Meanwhile,

(8) Lisa was having to give up her three beloved dogs, who had been like children to her, and a joy in their marriage together. After numerous calls, help from friends, homes were remarkably found for all three dogs.

But, now it moves to the "movie, book" level. The next e-mail that Lisa intercepted from

(9) girlfriend to Timothy, had info that the two of them had gotten married on July 17th in Ames, IA. He had met girlfriend the end of March, conned her, lied saying he was divorced in 2005. IA doesn't require proof of divorce to marry. (8) So, now we move into the legal system. Bigamy is a felony.

Lisa and I moved quickly, getting IA marriage license info on 2nd wedding while still married, police reports in IA, contact with DA office out there, contact with local police dept. Timothy and Amanda were brought in for questioning,

(11) he was arrested on Mon, the 27th.

(12) Meanwhile, Lisa is having to try to function and get school year started, always a demanding, challenging

time getting room ready, open house for parents, teacher planning meetings, kids start next week.

RESULT OF 2-3 EXTREMELY TRAUMATIC WEEKS

Lisa is extremely anxious, not eating, not sleeping. Body is wound tight, frequently shaking. Life went from normal to totally upside down with conning, deceit, craziness in a three week time, with her losing everything that she has spent years and years of hard working building and accomplishing. The total craziness of the mind rape of this is almost impossible to wrap the mind around.

She needs medication immediately for the high anxiety that has her body in a knot and medication to be able to sleep.

Her trying the Ambien CR is not working for her, she thinks due to the high anxiety. She is also gluten intolerant, which is adding to the eating challenges. I am very concerned about it being this long without sleep and blow after blow after blow. As a Licensed Professional Counselor myself and working in the field, I am well aware of the importance of medication right now to help her survive all of this insanity. Timothy, her seemingly charming and loving husband, appears to be a very skillful, cruel, talented con artist, perhaps sociopath, even though I'd never thought so before.

143

The whole thing leaves all of us in the family stunned in disbelief and aching for Lisa. She needs all the help and support she can get. The psychological thing of this is going to be huge for her to try to deal with and heal from. The mind games are chilling in their cruelty. For example, Timothy making plans with Lisa to go to GA coast July 18th and 19th, acting like things were fine, all the while he knew he was deserting her, walking out the door to marry another on July 17th, in IA, and then leaving the country for Uganda, to disappear and run from all the debt he had created and left behind for Lisa to deal with. Unreal.

Thank you for your help. It is very, very needed. If you have any questions, please feel free to contact me. Her father and I are teaming to help support Lisa through this nightmarish hell that dropped on her like a bomb with a text message July 11th, ending her life as she has known it.

Respectfully,

"Lisa's Mom"

I still think the doctor thought I was crazy, delusional. Who could blame her? The story sounded crazy coming from my lips. She probed, trying to ascertain the extent of my mental trouble.

"Do you hear voices?"

"No."

"Do you find yourself repeating behaviors or thoughts?"

"No."

"Do you feel like you want to hurt yourself?"

"No."

So far, so good.

Then came the cognitive assessment.

"Spell "world" forward and backwards."

"w-o-r-l-d. d-o-r-l...w. That's not right."

I knew it was wrong, not that I could not figure it out even as I re-rehearsed it in my head. I was certainly not ready for any spelling bees. She interrupted my mental spell-check with another command.

"Start from one hundred and count backwards by sevens."

I started confidently. "100, 93, 86, 79, 72."

Still confident, "63, 56, 49, 42, 35, 21..." I realized midstream that I had switched to the multiples of seven. Not very impressive for an advanced math teacher.

I wasn't suicidal. I wasn't obsessive. I wasn't psychotic. My cognitive impairment was temporary. All I wanted was relief from the insistent grip of anxiety, a night where sleep was not an elusive wish, a moment without my gut clenched in a ball. I wanted the numbness to fade, the shock to wear off. I wanted to inhabit my body once again.

I expressed to her my concern about medications. Although I had never shown any tendency towards addiction, I was afraid that in my weakened state, it would be all too easy for me to become dependent upon chemical soothers. I clarified that I wasn't experiencing any depression, but that the anxiety was crippling. She prescribed 20 mg of Celexa, as she was not comfortable neglecting an anti-depressant in my current situation, 1 mg Risperdal to aide in eating and to calm the tremors, and Trazodone to bring much-needed sleep. The latter would be an indicator of just how severely the trauma impacted my body. I was instructed to start with 50 mg at bedtime and to increase the dosage until I found that amount that would take down the barriers to sleep. I ended up at 300 mg, the maximum single dosage allowed in an outpatient situation.

The doctor-prescribed medications helped to ward off the demons of despair; they were potions to alleviate the agony of anxiety, and drugs to bring the first soothing slivers of slumber. The shaking slowly faded, the grip on the gut relaxed slightly, and the long nights became more bearable as the drugs manipulated my neurotransmitters, whispering platitudes and carrying away some of the awful weight. I slowly began to move back into my body, and the numbness was replaced with a strange sense of false calm. The Rube-Goldberg machines making up my mind began their action once again, their frenetic activity only occasionally misfiring. I wasn't healed, but I was functional yet again. An outdated model held together with patchwork repairs until a replacement could be found.

I was buoyed by the humor, cradled by the provided home, supported by my parents, and put back in running order with medications. Without all of those supports, I would not have made it through.

There is no shame is asking for help. We accept the fact that those at the end of life and those at the beginning of life require assistance, yet we somehow believe that adults should be able to be independent in spite of hardship. Divorce is the death of one life and the infancy of another. You will need help.

It is far better to temporarily suffer the embarrassment and discomfort of asking for help than to permanently suffer in silence. Ask for a hand, and let it guide you through.

Lessons From the End of a Marriage

Lesson Six

Tether yourself, so you do not lose yourself.

There were times I began to doubt my own sanity. His lies were strange and the truth stranger. I felt like Alice down that rabbit hole, unsure of the normal boundaries that hold life together. My synaptic junctions stuttered under the strain of comprehension. I was trying to come to terms with the fact that my entire life had been unknowingly built upon a bedrock of pumice.

My mom and I left for the airport at three in the morning. We were exhausted, neither one of us had slept much the night before, but we were also excited. It felt good to have a purpose, a definable goal: retrieve the car and move it back to Georgia. It was a task with an end.

As the plane descended over Iowa, I gazed down at the landscape that had welcomed Timothy so many times over the preceding months. I looked for answers in the fields, reasons for his betrayals in the rows of corn, signs in the Midwestern soil of why my husband had left. The crops were silent; I was closer to the crime, but no closer to explanations.

Upon arrival, we learned that he had been bailed out of jail the night before by his father, who wired money from Atlanta. I was enraged that he slipped out so quickly and surprised that his estranged father came to his rescue.

As we disembarked the plane, I realized that Timothy could be in the airport catching a flight back to Atlanta. I found myself scanning every face, every silhouette, looking for him. My breath caught every time I glimpsed a reasonable facsimile. I told myself I did not want to see him; I may have been lying.

My anxiety grew to a crescendo as we boarded the hour-long shuttle ride from the airport to Ames. The distance had provided some sort of protection from reality. Every mile stripped away some of my armor. I would have to face his wife and the city that hosted their betrothal unaided by a protective shield.

Driving down the streets of Ames, I matched the names of businesses and locations of ATM machines with activity on the checking account. It was as if Ames was a stranger to me, but I was familiar with its online profile. Likes: dinners out, large ATM withdrawals, and illicit affairs. Dislikes: responsible spending, paying bills, ethical behavior. As Ames and I met, I shed the last vestiges of the carapace that were protecting me from the truth. I had to face the source of my torment, the host of the deceptions. Ames and I reached an uneasy truce: it would not reveal more than I could bear and I would not hold the actions of a few of its citizens against it.

The shuttle dropped us off outside a Holiday Inn in town. I arranged for the officer to meet us at the hotel and take us to the impound lot that was hiding Timothy's car. I wondered what my hero looked like. What kind of eyes narrowed at Timothy's lies? What kind of hands snapped the handcuffs around Timothy's wrists? What kind of man moved in to protect me by arresting my husband?

He exuded a friendly confidence from his tall, slender frame. His presence immediately lowered my fear; I felt like I was in very capable hands. Within minutes, I was taking my first ride in the back of a police car. I pictured Timothy in the same seat, being transported into a future forever changed by his misdeeds.

One of my fears was that Timothy would get to his car before we could, rendering our trip to Iowa useless. I had nothing to worry about; Ben had ensured that Timothy would never have been able to locate his car; the impound lot was behind a tall fence in a residential neighborhood. Further protection was provided by the impound workers; they offered me a budget rate, but had a less wallet-friendly price in mind for Timothy, should he show up to try to claim his vehicle. I loved the fact that even these guys were on my side.

My mom and I sat in the police car with the officer while waiting for the Toyota to be retrieved from its hiding place. My mom's phone announced an incoming call from my dad. I had asked him to keep an eye on the joint checking account throughout the day. I expected Timothy's paycheck to be deposited sometime that morning, and I had instructed my dad to try to make a payment on the Toyota when the funds became available. This would serve the dual purpose of paying a needed bill while ensuring that Timothy would not have access to his full paycheck. My dad was calling to report that Timothy had beat him to the account; $500 had been withdrawn from an ATM in Ames. My mom relayed the address of the ATM to the inhabitants of the car. The officer immediately determined that Timothy must have spent the night at a downtown hotel. This information would become critical within the hour.

My stomach lurched as the Toyota pulled up behind the squad car. Timothy had occupied the vehicle a scant 24 hours earlier. As my mom played with the controls, learning the peculiarities of the vehicle,

I opened every compartment looking for clues, for answers. I found a copy of the Iowa marriage certificate. On it, Timothy had indicated that he and I divorced on September 5, 2005. Also of note was the fact that he checked the box indicating that he had a Bachelor's degree; Timothy barely earned his high school diploma.

In the glove compartment, behind my Suduko book that used to keep me calm in Atlanta traffic, was a familiar auto insurance card. Familiar except for one thing. I pulled my copy out of my purse and looked at them side by side. They were identical except mine had both of our names on it and his copy only had his name. Later, when I had access to a computer, I pulled up the PDF of the file on the insurance company's website. Sure enough, the official version had both names. Yet another example of Timothy's prowess with Photoshop and the extent to which he had gone to create an entirely new existence. It was frightening to hold that slip of paper in my hand; it was visceral evidence of the fact that I was married to a conman.

I learned about the ceremony from a to-do list and a rental agreement found in the center console of the Toyota. A 20' by 20' canopy provided shelter from the sun and any potential showers. The affair was catered by India Palace with three vegetarian dishes and one meat entrée. One hundred vegan cupcakes served as dessert. Lemonade and beer were served as refreshments for the guests. The ceremony began at 6:00 p.m., followed by water balloon fights, slip and sliding, and kite flying to the music of the Sunflower Field. A piñata was broken open around 7:30 p.m. before the band played their second set. At 9:00 p.m., the park was cleaned up and the revelers moved their festivities to a bar. There was only one thing missing: friends and family of the groom. I wonder if anyone found that strange.

Under the wedding plans, I found three small, wrinkled sheets of paper folded around an index card. They contained Timothy's wedding vows, written in his own hand.

> *I stand before you as your partner and friend your lover and companion for life. I pledge my undying loyalty to you – to stand by your side and support you during the best and worst that life may throw our way. I love you and I will always be there to laugh, love, and live a full life together.*

I wondered if these vows were any more authentic than the ones written and read to me ten years previously.

Once we finished uncovering the secrets held within the car, we followed the officer through the rain swept streets to the police station.

As we pulled into the police station in Timothy's vehicle, we saw the officer busy on his phone and his radio, ducking under the awning of the station for protection from the steady downpour. He had received a panicked call from Amanda; Timothy had sent her a text that stated he intended to end his life. He did not tell her his location.

As a result of my dad's earlier call, when the suicide call came in, Ben had a way to locate Timothy. The police and EMS were already on their way to the hotel where he was suspected to be staying.

My body did not respond. For two hours I did not know if my husband was alive or dead and my body did not respond. The man I loved and cherished was already dead; I did not care what happened to the man behind the mask. We sat in a conference room with the officer, completing paperwork, asking questions, and generally getting to know one another. The suicide drama continued with occasional radio updates. We learned that he had taken an overdose of over-the-counter sleeping pills and was losing consciousness when the police entered the hotel room. Conscienceness had already been lost.

I was able to read Timothy's statement, written that previous weekend prior to his arrest. His pleas for compassion bringing bile to my throat. His tone was whiney as he said he was just trying to find happiness. His signature was familiar, but the rest of document was written in an unknown hand. Apparently, he had assumed new handwriting along with his new wife and new life. I ran my fingers over his words, as though there was truth to be found in the ink. It kept its lips sealed.

We followed the officer again, this time to the main police department. He led us to the property room where Timothy's computers and computer bag were located. I was surprised to see his employer's property there; I was sure that he had sold it to fund his escape. The computer was not gone for good, but I was sure that his boss would not be thrilled with its current location.

The purpose of the visit to the property locker was to retrieve Timothy's hypertension medication (which he had stopped taking a week previously) at the request of the hospital. His heart must still be beating.

I rifled through the contents of his bag, taking the medication and inventorying what I found. There was a digital camera that I had never seen; I chose not to view the images. There was a wallet that only contained the credit cards that were maxed out, as well as the cards of which I was not aware (of course, these were maxed out by this point, too). He apparently had been maintaining two separate wallets. I frequently accessed the one I knew and had never seen these contents.

Two cameras. Two wallets. Two auto insurance cards. I wondered if he had maintained two phones as well since he always allowed me free access to his iPhone. There was no doubt he had been living two lives.

His contact case and glasses were in the bag; at this point, he had had his contacts in for over forty-eight hours. I left the vision supplies in his bag. I figured the hospital could provide him with a case and solution, and the loss of his sight would help to make him more vulnerable.

I hoped to find answers in Iowa. All I got were more questions.

The officer led us through the maze of the courthouse to the district attorney's office. We were greeted by his mom, who worked in the office. She was happy to hear us brag on her boy. We were taken to talk to the victim advocate and witness coordinator. I never knew there was such a position. The office looked out over the park where Timothy and Amanda were married just days before.

Legal system 101. A class I never wanted to take. I hoped I would earn a passing mark.

We learned that there would be several court dates leading up to the trial. His first appearance was scheduled for August 10, where he would be formally charged with bigamy. We were shown a chart that depicted the possible sentences based on number of prior convictions and current charge. In Iowa, bigamy is a class E felony, the lowest level. Because Timothy had no prior convictions, he would only be facing five to seven months' probation. As much as I was enjoying fantasies of his life in prison, I was not surprised at the sentence range. I emphasized that my priority was that he had to move forward in life with a felony conviction on his record. I could not live with the thought that he could plead it down to a misdemeanor.

While we were meeting with the victim coordinator, Ben went to personally deliver the medications to Timothy in the hospital. He had not returned by the time my mom and I were finished with our business, so we moved into the lobby of the district attorney's office to wait for him.

My mom took advantage of the pause in action to check her e-mails. I was jolted out of my daydream (yes, Timothy in prison stripes) when I heard her exclaim. I glanced at the screen on her phone, shocked to see Timothy's name attached to a message in her inbox. I immediately grabbed the phone from her hands, and paid no heed to the subject line.

Subject: Read this and then erase it - I don't think you should share this with Lisa unless you think this will give her some closure

I immediately knew that this had to be some sort of suicide letter. I had no idea that its contents would continue to haunt me.

Subject: Read this and then erase it - I don't think you should share this with Lisa unless you think this will give her some closure

Date: Tue, 28 Jul 2009 12:02:29 -0500

From: Timothy

To: Cathy Arends

CC: Amanda

By the time you get this I expect I will already be gone for good. I guess I just need somebody I can open up to right now before I close this final chapter for ever. First and most importantly - my feeble defense. Lisa is not the easiest person to live with (but hey! neither was I!). I lived a life with a woman who saw everyday as another problem. Can you imagine living a life with a person with whom day in and out saw life as misery and seemed to desperately need for me to feel the same way. This has been going on for many, many years. Ever since Lisa self diagnosed herself with shingles she has been suffering from colds, illness, aches, stress and a cadre of other problems that she just tells me I can't understand. For years I have been sharing my life with a woman that only seems to be happy when she's letting you know just how miserable she is. For years I worked every hour of overtime and took on every job I could so she could have the freedom to try and find whatever might bring her some shred of happiness. I gave up my life to work like a machine so she could have everything she needed to be happy only to just be reminded how unhappy and awful life is. When I broke down to Lisa a few months ago she asked me if I might be depressed - ha! I've been depressed and contemplating suicide for years! You would think that years spent sleeping in different rooms would have been some indication.

157

I hope this is coming across so that this makes some sense. I have lost everything. Yes I am guilty of leaving Lisa in the worst way possible and yes I am a coward but I didn't create the mess that she will unfortunately have to work with on her own. Did you know that your daughter isn't the world's most responsible spender? This isn't entirely her fault as I should have just cut up the credit cards and screamed "NO MORE!!". I always just thought that if my bonuses kept coming I might be able to keep up with the tremendous amount of money we were throwing out the door each month. I think things truly came to a head for me when Lisa self diagnosed herself with Celiac. Suddenly our $80 grocery bill jumped to a staggering $250 in which I was buying cheap seltzer water and bargain rate prepackaged sliced turkey. I have never been able to say no to Lisa. When she had to have a giant deck and an enormous hot tub I eventually gave in. When she had to have thousands of dollars in deck furniture I gave in to the pressure. When everything was done with the deck and suddenly she was under more pressure and had to go on vacation even though she promised me the deck would be the end of the spending spree. I eventually just caved and gave in. Look at the pictures on my laptop - do I really look happy? I would send you the pictures but I have nothing but the clothes I'm wearing and my phone. Please let Lisa know that the password to my laptop is mondoabo42 and the password to the DS computer is monkeybone. The DS computer is just that - a work machine. My laptop is whatever she wants. It holds the scraps of what was my life and I hope she smashes it into *tiny little pieces because that machine brought me more happiness than I have felt in a great many years. I had thought today that I would be able to take my equipment and the DS gear pack it into my car and move to Michigan to try and save my job. As Lisa has seen fit to tell the police to take everything from me then even that little shred of hope is even gone. I meant what I said in my letter - I would have worked for the rest of my life to help Lisa to pay off OUR debt. I want to be completely clear in this matter as my arresting officer asked a question that could only have come from one place. I didn't steal and hide anything. I didn't empty out our account and hide the funds someplace else. To do what I have done I cashed in my retirement funds to try and live this little dream. I knew it would come to an unpleasant ending but I had hoped that everybody wouldn't turn against me. It's ironic that I would turn to you to share my tale as your daughter has done nothing but complain about you but you can think of this as my find confession - my last rights. You somehow seemed to be the right person to share with.*

I would like to share my love and time with Amanda. Christ.... How do I explain myself. Yes. I love her. Yes I have given up everything for this amazing woman. Yes. I am damned all the more for it. I met the amazing woman in Las Vegas while I was working a show in March. I was feeling especially low after an awful night spent pretending to enjoy the company of people who cared for nothing but themselves. To be honest - I was looking for an end that night. Instead after walking for a few hours I stepped into a little bar to listen to a bit of music and met the last bit of happiness of my life. She just seemed to glow to me from across the room. Maybe it was her smile or her eyes - hell it was probably both that both drew me to her and scared me half to death. I kept trying to work up the courage to leave when I looked across the room and found her right in front of me. All thoughts of flight left my mind at that moment and I was suddenly desperate to talk to this amazing woman. Let me be clear at this point - I have been on the road for a very, very long time and have spoken to many women of the course of my travels. Never have I ever cheated. As these are my final words I can and will say and tell whatever I want and damn the world if you don't believe me. This woman was different. I wish I could explain to you why my dear reader but there was something magical about her. I met this woman in the sinkhole that is Vegas only to learn that she understood my stupid sense of humor and enjoyed my company. Even more importantly she was vastly smarter than me and didn't rub it in my face. I wish you could meet her - she is without a doubt the most incredible and intensely amazing person I have ever met in all of my travels and somebody I am proud to have shared my final moments with. My relationship with her was the best and happiest I have been in..... it was the happiest I have ever been and now it's over. I wish that I could have some closure with her before I have to do this awful thing to myself. I wish to everything that is good and right in the world that she didn't turn her back on me the way she did. I gave up everything and now I am left by myself with just this one awful answer to all of my problems. I love Amanda because she gave me the only hope and happiness I have had in too many years. Now I end my life because in the end we simply die alone with nobody to care.

I would have sent this tonight but the razor in my room wasn't up to the job of finishing this nasty task. I will send this all later this morning as soon as I can secure the proper tools to end my life. I didn't want this but I am left alone and hopeless. The only people I have ever cared about in my life all want me dead - at least I can bring them some comfort by making this happen.

I'm sorry for unloading this on you but I needed to share with somebody before I left for the eternal darkness. I know what waits for me after this life - nothing. Eternal and everlasting emptiness. Who knows - maybe some scrap of me still lingers on afterwards to ponder life's greatest questions or maybe I will wind up in a world of eternal hell and damnation. But then really - who cares what happens to me. I will die alone. We all die alone.

Be well Cathy. I'm sorry for emptying my soul to you but I had no place else to turn. Please help Lisa through these hard times and never tell her of this letter. If you ever have a chance to meet Amanda I know you understand just how amazing she really is as how crushed I am to lose her. I can't live without her and she thinks of me only as a monster. Was I really so wrong to want to try and find happiness in my life? I guess the final answer is yes.

May you live in peace. Please forget me - I was never worth anything anyway.

In the end I know that nobody ever really cared about me - they just cared about what I could do for them. I just wish I could have done something for myself over the years to try and find true happiness.

Tim

The lies.

The whole letter was full of lies.

He continued to try to destroy me; his intent to discredit me from beyond the grave.

Would anybody believe me now? I felt repulsion towards him as the impact of his words began to sink in to my core.

The staccato leg retuned full force; my entire body trembled once again. I felt sick as I tried to come to terms with the contents of the letter. There were many true assessments Timothy could have made about me. I was too intense, possessing an on/off switch in place of a dial. I was prone to anxiety, which led me to worry and at times would make me too conservative and careful. I worked too much and could become hyper-focused on a task or to-do list. These would have been valid complaints. Complaints he didn't make. Rather, he made absurd claims. Attacks that didn't even make sense. The attacks were peppered with strange statements, such as he loved Amanda because, "She let me be myself." Uhmm...did he conveniently forget that their entire relationship was built on his lies?

Ben returned from dropping off the medication to Timothy's hospital room. I held my mom's iPhone out to him so that he could read the e-mail. He chuckled. I looked up, shocked. What in the world was funny?

"He CC'd Amanda. This was done to try to win her back. She's at the hospital with him now."

The contents of the e-mail, soon to be dubbed "The Last Con Letter," still stung with the power of a thousand wasps, but I welcomed Ben's perspective. I had indeed missed Amanda's name at the top. I do not know if his suicide attempt was sincere, but it seemed as though he was laying the groundwork to manipulate it for his gain if he survived. His plans worked. Amanda, who had left him only days before thankful for her survival, was now back by his side.

The Last Con Letter sent my mind into a tailspin. Recent memories kept forcing their way into the front of my cortex where they would contrast with what I now knew.

As I gained new information, I began to comprehend how my reality of the past several years was actually a carefully crafted normalcy, deliberately woven and draped to cover the lies. The stark contrast between what was and what appeared to be was highlighted by my newfound knowledge.

Flashbacks of recent events flashed across my mind like sharp bolts of lightening, illuminating and deadly, highlighting his lies against a murky backdrop. Each memory brought insight and clarity paired with pain. I was no closer to understanding how he could do what he did, but the utter cruelty and complexity of it became clear. These thoughts were random, struck out of nowhere and bypassed my defenses.

Our home phone line stopped working in the January of 2009. Timothy spent $50 and two days trying to locate the source of the problem, but was unable to repair the line. This correlated with when he stopped keeping up with the bills; cutting the phone line would keep me in the dark a while longer. As a result of the disconnected phone line, I was without a working alarm system while Timothy was out of town with Amanda. He risked my safety to hide his deceit.

On the night that Timothy broke down in May, I asked him if there was anyone else. He replied, "No, never. I would never do that to you."

He had met Amanda five weeks earlier.

On of the slips of paper from June, I wrote, "I love when you confide in me." He read that note while we were both in the kitchen. He moved up behind me, slid his arms around me and whispered in my ear,

"I always confide in you."

Timothy had put on quite a bit of weight from 2006 to 2008. In the summer of 2008, he began to exercise more frequently and watched what he ate. As a result, he lost over fifty pounds over the next year. He was looking good, and beginning to take pride in his developing physique. I was happy when he decided on a new, sexier style of underwear in May of 2009. I went with him to several store locations to find enough pairs in his size. I even checked the store while he was in Brazil. The underwear change was for Amanda's benefit.

A week before leaving for Brazil, Timothy took a jacket to a tailor. It was part of the suit that he wore for our wedding almost ten years ago. It was the same jacket he wore when he wed Amanda, the fabric witness to false oaths. I never saw him in the newly tailored jacket.

Timothy woke with me before dawn on July 5 to take me to the airport to catch my flight to Seattle. I was excited about the trip, but I wasn't ready to be away from Timothy again.

Holding me closely at the entrance to the security line, he said, "Don't worry. The week will go quickly. You'll be back before you know it."

"I know," I replied, "But I'm still going to miss you."

"Unlike Brazil, we'll be able to talk every day," he reassured me.

"Promise?"

"I'll contact you so much you won't know what to do."

These words were punctuated by passionate kisses as we prepared to say our goodbyes. He knew that it was goodbye forever.

Timothy kept his word about frequent contact. The text messages started before I even made it to the gate.

Love ya!!! Have a smooth flight and be safe!

So much for mowing the grass today – it's already sprinkling!! Love ya!

Hi there thumbs

How was your three minute jaunt through security?

I told ya I'd stay in touch!

I should be funny and text you "are you there yet?" every five minutes!

Love you!!!

Welcome to Seattle!

I talked to him every day while I was in Seattle. My dad said he could always tell when I was on the phone with Timothy because I would laugh so much, my giggles echoing through the house. He must have been packing in between sending these messages.

While I was in Seattle, we talked about a Best Buy bill I received when Timothy was in Brazil. He told me that he called on it and it was a case of identity theft. We were no strangers to this crime; he had his identity stolen from apartment records soon after we moved to Atlanta. He suggested that we pull our credit reports again to check to see if there was any other suspicious activity. I agreed. It had been a few years since we last pursued our reports.

The bankruptcy attorney pulled my report ten days later. The only suspicious activity on the accounts was done by Timothy.

My mom added a new word to her vocabulary in July: fuck. As in mindfuck, the only word that could begin to capture the feeling of the psyche coming to terms with the complex con. One question dominated my mind in the days following the suicide attempt: did he have a conscience? If yes, then how could he hurt those closest to him so deeply and continue to inflict pain through his piercing words? If no, how did he keep up the act for sixteen years and create such a powerful illusion of forming bonds with me and with the dogs? Neither option brought peace, but the lack of a conscience answered all of the "why" questions that had been plaguing me for weeks and carried with it some understanding. Was that *the* answer? If so, did he always lack a conscience, or, as he implied in his confession, did he lose it at some point along the way? Even answers brought more questions.

I had been living in a virtual reality. The goggles had been violently ripped off, leaving me blinking in the harsh light, trying to orient myself in my new world. I no longer had any sense of what was real and what was manufactured. I felt like one of the humans in *The Matrix*, released from the mechanized puppet masters, struggling with the news that they had simply been fuel for the lies.

In trying to keep me in the dark, Timothy lost himself. I would have to tether myself to reality, so that I did not lose myself in the process.

"Dear John" Letter Fifth Interpretation (July 27, 2009)

Lisa,

I'm afraid there is no easy way for me to say this – I'm leaving. *Pretty much got that part through my head by now.* We have had a long and rich life together but I can no longer live this life anymore. *What life would that be? The one you invented where I cheated on you with Mythical Mark Mercer? The one where you have told so many lies and spun so many tales that you can no longer speak the truth to anyone? YOU are the one who created that life over the past few years. YOU are the one who hid that life from me and everyone else around you. I can't muster any sympathy for you. I notice your use of the word, "rich." I wonder what you mean by that. The context implies emotional depth and fulfillment. In retrospect, that certainly has not been the case for years: you were pretending and I was an uninformed actor in your play. Or, do you mean financially rich? We both worked so hard to get where we were and took pride in the fact that we were never dependent upon others financially. You undermined that with your unrestrained spending. Did you intentionally sabotage what we had worked for? Regardless of your motives or non-motives, we are now both dependent upon others for financial solvency.* As I told you several months ago, I feel as though we have been drifting apart for a number of years. *Now dear, I don't think drifting is the proper word choice. Drifting implies aimless motion, occurring when attention wanders. Your attentions were deliberately misrouted; mine were focused on a sham. Drifting also gives the impression of mutual fault. This one lies solely on you.*

It was a gradual thing but I can honestly say that it has reached a point where I no longer can share time with you without wondering when I can be away from you again.

Gradual? I'm thinking more...

Downward spiral

Inevitable decline

Exponential decay

Terminal velocity

Strapped in and no way out

You had no boundaries, no depths you refused to reach. You were on a collision course with hell. The sting of the latter part of that sentence is lessening; I no longer feel the stab as a personal affront. You knew your lies were being sniffed out. You knew you couldn't hide much longer. I can't keep living this lie – it's not fair to either one of us. *First off, it is "lies," not "lie." Keep your tenses straight. Secondly, not fair to you? It does not seem like that has been a concern of yours.* I will continue to support you as best I can from wherever I end up. *So you call bleeding the account within two days of each paycheck "support"? You are delusional. For the record, I do not find your dinners with Amanda supportive.* I will continue to work for DS but I would appreciate if you didn't involve them in this matter. *Hmm…you are going to still work for them, but you sold their equipment? Interesting method for advancement in the workplace. I bet you don't want me to involve them. That had to be really awkward when I called asking why you hadn't yet returned from Brazil. Oops.* We had some amazing times together and I will treasure these memories for the rest of my life. *So that is why any mementos or pictures of me were left behind?* I think people change as they experience life and unfortunately we have grown so far apart that I simply cannot relate to you in any way. *Right about now, I would have to say that feeling is entirely mutual. Who the hell are you?*

I know that this will hit you very hard and for that I am sincerely sorry. *Sincere? When have you ever been sincere about anything? For a con artist, you sure like to use those "trust" words. Too bad the actions don't match.* I have never wanted to do anything to harm you in any way but in doing so I have made myself unhappy for many years. *Uh...poor baby?* I know that once you recover from the shock of this you will bounce back and live a happy and satisfying life – a better and more honest life than I could ever hope to offer you. *Bouncing – yeah that's what I'm doing.* Everything I have left behind is yours and all I have taken is my clothing and the equipment I need to make a living. *And the birth certificate you needed to get married.* I will never ask you for forgiveness or understanding. *Blah ,blah, blah.* I am a coward who couldn't tell you to your face that I am leaving. *Or tell me to my face that you were getting married. That would be an unusual conversation.* If I don't do this now then I probably never will. *Never will what? Commit bigamy? Move to Africa?* I need my life to have some sort of meaning to it and unfortunately working in the basement of my house and watching tv and playing video games isn't it. *You're right; prison is much more meaningful. And they don't let you have video games.*

I'm sorry but my life is very quickly becoming that of my parents. *Your dad did marry your mom before the divorce from his first wife was final. But again, at least he did not hide.* No matter how much I see that, it feels like there is nothing I can do to change the path that I am on. *You mean you HAD to get married? Again? Without a divorce? That is a strange path that will lead you straight to a felony.* From this point on there is nothing more that I can say other than how sorry I am for leaving you in this way. *Yeah, I have to agree that this is pretty fucked up.* I will do everything I can from this point forward to try and make this as easy on you as possible. *You're right. You could have written a book entitled "Divorce With Dignity."* I didn't strip the account to leave. *Now I see, you stripped it to get married. I had no money in Seattle due to your wedding ring and the cost of Amanda's outweighed a mortgage payment.* I sold everything downstairs that I felt was part of the old me that I so desperately need to leave behind. *Except your old wedding rings; I guess it was too inconvenient to deal with your first legal marriage – so much easier just to leave it behind as a remnant of life past.*

Lesson Seven

When someone hurts you, it is because they are in pain.

Those early weeks and months were saturated with anger. I had walked through the fire and I was still carrying the coals, and embers can still burn tender flesh. I seethed when I thought of him kissing me while his new vows sat waiting in his car. I roiled when I considered the years of velvet-trimmed lies whispered softly into trusting ears. I cursed his name, his very existence.

I saw each of his actions as being done deliberately to me; my prince turned into Machiavelli, carefully crafting a character assassination against me. I saw him purposefully plotting my destruction, looking for ways to harm me further, take me deeper, and pull the very essence of myself away from my bones.

That was my ego talking.

He was no more thinking of me when he made those choices than I was taking him into consideration as I was busy playing the angry victim.

I knew that I didn't want to be angry anymore long before I discovered how to let go of the anger. I didn't want to live with him as my persecutor, setting the tone for the rest of my days. The desire for vengeance kept me prisoner for a time, bars made with the steel of indignation holding my damaged self in a helpless cage. I let him keep me there. I sought validation, not freedom. I wanted to scream out, "Look what he did to me!" while pointing at the bars of my own making.

Eventually, I softened. The riverbed of time wearing away at the sharp knife edge of my pain and anger. My image of him changed as well. I was able to see him more clearly, not just as the attacker of our marriage, but as an individual in his own right. With his own pain.

The real shift came on a nondescript day riding a nondescript highway on the way into work. The thought entered my mind like a shot of caffeine, causing me to gasp and tremble with the impact. I saw him as a child. A child who had taken actions that he knew would cause displeasure and, in turn, cause him discomfort. Just as a child lies to protect himself, he lied to protect self, not harm another.

July 2009

We had left Iowa and we were slowly making our way back to Atlanta in the Toyota. Our first night was spent at a retreat center not far from the state line. I spent hours that evening walking the paths that crossed the property while talking with my dad. I was shaken by Timothy's e-mail sent to my mom. It was filled with nothing but lies, but it still shook me. I didn't understand how he could hurt me so badly and then claim it was my fault. I'd already received a rejection letter; I didn't think it required a follow up.

I knew from the police that Timothy's parents were driving up from Atlanta to take him home from the hospital where he was still in ICU from his uncontrolled hypertension and his suicide attempt. I decided to take a chance and call them to give them whatever information I could.

I had always had a pretty good relationship with his mom. We used to spend quite a bit of time together when Timothy and his dad were working or out of town. They settled just two streets over from us outside of Atlanta and, for years, we would go over for a family dinner every Sunday at 4:00 p.m. His parents were always sure to have enough vegetarian dishes for me and his dad would make me huge batches of my favorite mashed potatoes. After drinking heavily through much of Timothy's childhood, they had both quit by the time we were married. The damage had already been done, however, and he and his parents never really knew how to relate to each other. Around 2007, Timothy decided that he did not want to go over there any more and he pulled back almost all contact with them. I never knew why, but, as they were his parents, I honored his wishes.

His mom sounded surprised to hear from me, but grateful. The only information they had came from the police. I ran through the story. I was getting good at telling it now. She kept breaking in,

"Oh my God, Lisa. I'm so sorry."

They were as shocked in this as everyone else, more collateral damage on his collision course. Their only plan at the moment was to pick him up and get him back to their place. We talked about the need for psychiatric care for him. I let them go as they arrived at the hospital. She promised to call me back later. I never heard from her nor saw her again.

Between the shock of the suicide letter and the emotions associated with talking with his mom, I was teeming with anxiety again.

I took a Xanax to sleep that night. One of only three I would take in the coming months.

The second leg of the journey took us to Nashville, where we were to spend one more night before returning to Atlanta.

We were five miles from the exit for the hotel when my mom's phone rang.

Timothy's name flashed on the screen.

"What do I do?" I asked, shocked at seeing his name on the screen. I was prepared to never hear from him again; I was not ready for this.

"Don't answer it," she replied, equally stunned.

We sat silently as the phone continued to ring. A chime soon announced a new voice mail. I pulled the headphones out of her purse to listen to the message. He sounded strange, dead, defeated. He stated that he needed help and needed to talk with someone.

As we were discussing the proper course of action, the phone announced the following text from Timothy:

I need to talk to you. I want to try and start making things right. I know that I have destroyed everything but I also know that I can also work on making things right. Yesterday I felt like I couldn't handle things anymore - please help to give me a chance to be responsible. I need help but I can also help as well.

7/29/2009

7:56 PM

I was shocked.

My mom was not.

She explained that it is not uncommon to have a narrow window of opportunity after a serious suicide attempt.

My patience was tested as I helped her navigate to a hotel near the interstate. We checked in, placed our belongings in the room, and discussed the appropriate response all the while.

I did not feel right not responding to a suicidal person asking for help.

My mom was torn – the counselor in her wanted to help; the mother in her was ready to lash out to protect her young.

What do you have in mind?

7/29/2009

8:10 PM

She suggested the following, which I quickly typed and sent.

We left the hotel to visit a nearby grocery store to obtain dinner. The phone did not leave my hand as I anxiously waited for a response. His reply came while we were in the personal care aisle.

Whatever it takes. Please just give me some way to help. I didn't think that I would wake up again today. When I did I understood that I can't avoid reality. I need help but I can help too. I just need a way.

7/29/2009

8:27 PM

My mom verbally composed her retort while selecting a frizz-fighting mousse. Again, I typed her response, assuming my role as the translator.

What do you see as reality?

7/29/2009

8:29 PM

His response came faster this time. We paused in frozen foods.

Responsibility.

7/29/2009

8:30 PM

What would taking responsibility look like at this time?

7/29/2009

8:31 PM

I've fallen apart and I'm trying to put myself together again. Please let me help to fix this.

7/29/2009

8:31 PM

Would it be wrong to make a Humpy Dumpty joke here?

My mom and I were looking for the wine. Apparently, grocery stores in Tennessee are not allowed to sell alcohol of any kind. We moved to the check out line.

What are steps you're wanting to take to put things back together again?

7/29/2009

8:33 PM

I've destroyed our relationship but I can work to clean up the rest of the mess. To do that I need to be able help.

7/29/2009

8:35 PM

I need you and Lisa to tell me what I can do.

7/29/2009

8:35 PM

> ***I'm not sure what you mean by our***
> ***relationship? Yours and mine? Or you and***
> ***Lisa?***
>
> ***7/29/2009***
>
> ***8:37 PM***

We carried the groceries to the car and walked to a liquor store next door to find the much-needed bottle of wine.

> *Please give me a chance to at least clean this up. I tried to take a very cowardly way out yesterday and very nearly succeeded let me work to be responsible again.*
>
> *7/29/2009*
>
> *8:44 PM*
>
> *Both. Everything. I need help and I need to be able to help too.*
>
> *7/29/2009*
>
> *8:46 PM*
>
> *I'm not asking for a second chance but just some way to work towards making things right.*
>
> *7/29/2009*
>
> *8:47 PM*

Specifically, what do you think would be responsible choices at this time?

7/29/2009

8:47 PM

Entering the liquor store, a wine display immediately caught our eye: *Ménage a Tois*. Somehow that seemed like the perfect vintage for the evening.

Financial. I will agree to almost anything and then leave to work in Michigan if that is still an option. I will offer anything. I'm not a bad person - I've just gotten lost. I know that seems like a joke but give me some way to make this right.

7/29/2009

8:50 PM

Do you still have your job with DS?

7/29/2009

8:51 PM

A good first step would be to be completely honest about the current financial situation.

7/29/2009

8:54 PM

Back to the grocery store. Apparently, liquor stores in Tennessee are not allowed to sell bottle openers of any kind.

I don't know. Probably not if I can't get their computer back. If I can't keep my job I can't help. I'm already so lost - but I know that this is all because of the mistakes I've made. I couldn't deal with that yesterday but I can try to today.

7/29/2009

8:54 PM

No more stories. No more lies. I just want to be responsible. I will take the weight of this on my own shoulders.

7/29/2009

8:56 PM

Good thing he had been working out.

> **I expect you'll get your computer back at the first court date which I believe is August 10th.**
>
> **7/29/2009**
>
> **8:56 PM**

If that's true then I will lose what chance I have to help. I want to make things right.

7/29/2009

8:58 PM

> **Send an e-mail to Lisa's new e-mail address with a detailed list of debts, unpaid bills, IRS info, etc.**
>
> **7/29/2009**
>
> **9:00 PM**

I don't have her address on my phone. I'll put together a list - this list will be mine to deal with - not hers. There has to be someway we can do that. I'm not in the best condition right now but I will make a list tomorrow morning. I'm not putting this off but I'm still a mess from yesterday. I need to have a clear head as I put this together. I will take responsibility for it but I need my computer to keep my job so I can help. I'm a bastard but I want to make things right. I don't know how things got to this point in my life but can I have a chance to clean this up

7/29/2009

9:06 PM

That's why I'm putting this in writing.

7/29/2009

9:07 PM

We finally made it back to the hotel room with our loot. We microwaved our dinners, opened the bottle of wine, and sat down to a meal at a small hotel table. We continued the text conversation as we sipped the Chardonnay blend from plastic water cups.

You can e-mail it to me and I'll forward it to her. What is DS saying to you?

7/29/2009

9:08 PM

Let me show some responsibility.

7/29/2009

9:08 PM

I haven't spoken to them since yesterday or the day before. I can still barely talk.

7/29/2009

9:09 PM

Just help give me a way to fix this mess. I want to help Lisa not hurt her anymore than I already have.

7/29/2009

9:11 PM

Let me think about it. I'm going to be tied up for the next 15 minutes. Where are you right now?

7/29/2009

9:14 PM

I'm in a hotel with my parents. The hospital released me to their care. I know that I'm asking for a lot - that's why I'm putting this in writing. I'm not asking for a second chance - just a chance to take responsibility. Lisa doesn't deserve this and I can at least stand up and be responsible for all of this.

7/29/2009

9:17 PM

In writing? Everything he had said lately had been in writing. Does he think we believe that he is incapable of falsehoods while typing? The macabre humor crept in as we began to feel the effects of the wine. Each response brought questions: what was true? What was a lie? How much was being stated because he knew what others wanted to hear? Even though every answer was received with doubt, we still took advantage of the palaver to try to obtain some answers.

> **What are your plans now? Are you going back with your parents or are you going to Detroit?**
>
> **7/29/2009**
>
> **9:25 PM**

I'm going back with my parents for a few days with the hopes of cleaning things up. I'm going to ask DS to suspend me from the payroll until I get there. I'm going to start making things right again. I just wish I didn't have to try and kill myself to understand that. Let me be responsible again. Let me take the responsibility for this. I've hurt so many people and I need to start making things right again.

7/29/2009

9:29 PM

Time to contact Peewee's Playhouse; I guess "responsible" is the word of the day. We even joked about a drinking game hinging on his use of the word "responsibility," but we didn't have enough wine nor the constitutions for such quantities of alcohol.

I'm hearing your words of wanting to be responsible. How does that translate to action?

7/29/2009

9:31 PM

I will do whatever is necessary. If that means filling for bankruptcy or any thing else I will do it and carry the full weight of this. I will start looking at what I should start doing tomorrow so I can present either you or Lisa with solutions. I want to make this right.

7/29/2009

9:35 PM

When you have your list of solutions, send them to me and I'll forward them to Lisa.

7/29/2009

9:37 PM

I will. I know this doesn't help but I'm sorry and I want to make this right. I don't ask for forgiveness just the opportunity to make things right again.

7/29/2009

9:39 PM

Are there other computers you can use to do DS work until you get your computer back?

7/29/2009

9:41 PM

I wish to god there was. What little I have left to try and clean this up is on those computers. Without them I'm done.

7/29/2009

9:43 PM

Do you or DS have backups of any of that info?

7/29/2009

9:48 PM

Just what was with my computers.

7/29/2009

9:55 PM

There isn't any other backup

7/29/2009

9:56 PM

Sounds like you're really backed into a corner right now.

7/29/2009

9:57 PM

Yeah. I am.

7/29/2009

9:57 PM

But I built this corner and pushed myself into it.

7/29/2009

9:58 PM

That's true.

7/29/2009

9:59 PM

I know. I just want to start making this right. I didn't die yesterday for some reason. I don't know how the police found me. I'm awake again for the first time in a long time.

7/29/2009

10:08 PM

Should we tell him that we were the reason he was alive? Nah. It's more fun to let him think it was some sort of divine intervention.

How are you awake now that you weren't before?

7/29/2009

10:10 PM

Because now I can point at myself. Because now I'm not trying to pretend that everything is fine and that I'm fine too. I'm broken but someday I might be able to make something of myself again. Because now I can stand by the truth stop pretending that it's not there. Suicide has a way of making you see things you don't want to face.

7/29/2009

10:22 PM

What are you seeing now that you didn't want to face before?

7/29/2009

10:23 PM

Dear god. Where do I begin? That just because you want something doesn't mean that it will happen. That problems don't get better by ignoring them. Everything. I tried to create a world where I convinced myself that everything was somehow fine no matter how bad things looked. As crazy as it sounds I believed my own bullshit and just deluded myself into believing that everything could be ok. I can finally come to terms with that and start moving forward.

7/29/2009

10:29 PM

Sounds like you're learning some important things.

7/29/2009

10:30 PM

Yeah. I'm sorry I'm such a mess. I'm sorry for everything I've put you and Lisa through. I know that doesn't help anything but I have to at least have the chance to say it.

7/29/2009

10:36 PM

Wow. I got an apology. I wish I could believe that he truly meant it.

Yes, all choices have consequences.

_7/29/2009_

_10:39 PM_

I know. I am taking responsibility and taking control of my life again. I want to do everything in my power to work to make this right for Lisa again. No more bullshit.

_7/29/2009_

_10:44 PM_

Looks like "make this right" is in a close second to "responsibility."

How long have you been doing bullshit and why?

_7/29/2009_

_10:45 PM_

Lying about finances - years. Lying about our relationship since March. Yes I cheated on Lisa with Amanda. Yes I was unstable while I was doing this. Yes I had a drinking problem for years. I know I shouldn't put this into writing but I don't *care. I just want to move forward in a way that stops hurting Lisa.*

7/29/2009

10:50 PM

These lines, regardless of their veracity, lessened the sting of the "last con" letter. They also lined up with the information that I had been able to find. While he was in Brazil, I found empty bottles in a cabinet in the basement shop. That was my first sign that alcohol had become a problem. I never had time to confront him about it, but this clarified that drinking was a component of his actions.

What contributed to your being dishonest about finances for years?

7/29/2009

10:52 PM

I didn't die yesterday and there has to be some reason for that. Let this be it.

7/29/2009

10:52 PM

Good question. I wish I had a descent answer. My income has had peaks and flatlines. I think that when I started getting big bonuses for the work I was doing it suddenly seemed to feel all right to start spending irresponsibly. When I didn't get my last bonuses when I left (my previous employer) I just thought that I could find some other way to clean this up.

7/29/2009

10:55 PM

Ahhh, a lie here. He left his former company at the end of 2008, but the signs pointing to financial deceptions went back to at least 2005.

> **Yes, this is a time and opportunity to learn, to grow, and to be more honest with yourself and others.**
>
> **7/29/2009**
>
> **10:59 PM**

I want to do everything I can. I know that might not mean much coming from me right now but it's the truth. It's the only way I will be able to live with myself.

7/29/2009

11:04 PM

What stopped you from going to Lisa the
first time you pre-spent a bonus that
didn't show up?

7/29/2009

11:06 PM

Self delusion

7/29/2009

11:08 PM

Say more

7/29/2009

11:09 PM

I still held out some hope that promises might be kept. I
thought that if I could just stretch things out and keep
hammering (my previous employer) that I could get paid and
then things would be ok again. My last bonus would have
given me the freedom to either clean things up or just keep
digging a hole. I'd like to say that I would have taken a

responsible path then but I know I can now. I've been through too much.

7/29/2009

11:12 PM

It sounds like Timothy was learning Newton's First Law: an object tends to stay in the state it is in. I hoped he would soon become familiar with the third tenet: every action has an equal and opposite reaction as he faced the repercussions of a felony charge.

That's sad. The price now is tragically high for not being honest then.

7/29/2009

11:13 PM

I know. I'm a fool but I know. At least now I recognize what I've done and I can start working to make things right. I don't think that would have been possible before this morning.

7/29/2009

11:15 PM

**In what ways do you feel you've been a
fool?**

7/29/2009

11:17 PM

*Every. There is nothing responsible about how I've been living
my life. It's gone all the way to the point I'm in a cheap hotel
bed with my entire body shaking and on fire from what I did
yesterday*

7/29/2009

11:21 PM

**It sounds like this feels very different than
you're used to feeling.**

7/29/2009

11:24 PM

Yes

7/29/2009

11:25 PM

I'm taking control of my life again and being responsible about it

7/29/2009

11:25 PM

No more bullshit

7/29/2009

11:26 PM

All I ask is a bit of guidance to make sure that I'm not making any more mistakes.

7/29/2009

11:27 PM

When did doing bullshit become your way of being?

7/29/2009

11:27 PM

I really don't know. I just dug myself into a hole and tried to dig my way through to the other side. I never stopped to look around and ask for help. I know I need help. I can admit now that I am depressed and I have been for a long time.

7/29/2009

11:30 PM

What stopped you from asking for help?

7/29/2009

11:31 PM

I was scared and ashamed that I couldn't deal with this on my own. I've never known how to ask for help with anything.

7/29/2009

11:32 PM

It sounds like a big learning now is asking for help, which takes strength and courage.

7/29/2009

11:35 PM

I can't keep trying to deal with my problems by myself. I now know where that path will lead me to.

7/29/2009

11:39 PM

We finished the last of the wine.

You are so right.

7/29/2009

11:40 PM

I know that now. I just wish that I could have asked for help sooner. Yesterday this was too much to deal with and yet I still couldn't ask for help. I can now and I can start making things right.

7/29/2009

11:42 PM

The price of this has been tragically high for everyone.

7/29/2009

11:43 PM

I know and I'm sorry.

7/29/2009

11:44 PM

**And I sincerely hope that you will make
wiser and different choices in the future
and ask for help. Help is available.**

7/29/2009

11:45 PM

*I am and I will but I can't do this on my own. I need help. I
need somebody to talk to so I can understand where this all
comes from.*

7/29/2009

11:47 PM

**What are your thoughts on where it comes
from?**

7/29/2009

11:49 PM

I don't know yet but I can at least admit that it's there and ask for help. I'm hoping with time somebody can help me understand all of this.

7/29/2009

11:51 PM

That's very, very possible if you'll do your part.

7/29/2009

11:52 PM

I will. I want to be the person I used to be. I just need help to understand why I went down this road.

7/29/2009

11:54 PM

What did you used to be?

7/29/2009

11:55 PM

Honest and happy. Not just angry and bitter all the time.

7/29/2009

11:56 PM

We started to get ready for bed while we continued the conversation.

What happened?

7/29/2009

11:57 PM

I don't know. I'm hoping to better understand myself and the problems I have. I don't know how long that will take but I will invest the time to understand this.

7/29/2009

11:59 PM

When do you think it started?

7/30/2009

12:00 AM

I wish I knew. It was a slow process that built itself up over the years. I can't say there was any defining moment that started all of this.

7/30/2009

12:02 AM

So often that's exactly how it happens.

7/30/2009

12:03 AM

I just wish I could have asked for help sooner. I was afraid of what that would mean. I was scared to open myself up and admit that I need help with my problems.

7/30/2009

12:05 AM

Avoidance can result in so much loss for everyone. It's not the answer.

7/30/2009

12:07 AM

I know that now. I was just to blind to see that sooner.

7/30/2009

12:10 AM

What are Amanda's plans now?

7/30/2009

12:13 AM

She's leaving the state after my trial for California and then after that she's leaving for Uganda for a year.

7/30/2009

12:15 AM

What were your plans for Uganda?

7/30/2009

12:16 AM

There are none. My tentative plans are to head to Michigan so I can work to clean this up. I think for some crazy reason my boss might give me a chance. I've already texted back and forth a bit with him tonight to explain myself.

7/30/2009

12:22 AM

Service here is really bad. Sorry for the delays between answers but it takes a few tries to make a message go through.

7/30/2009

12:23 AM

This immediately jumped out as a falsehood; he frequently used this excuse from Brazil. I guess he wasn't really done with bullshit after all.

> **No, I'm talking past tense. Before everything caved in on you, what were your plans in Uganda?**
>
> **7/30/2009**
>
> **12:24 AM**

I never really got that far. I wanted to still manage my DS projects but I was genuinely excited about getting involved in volunteer work that could make a difference. It made me think of the work I used to do with James at the scout camp.

7/30/2009

12:28 AM

Now this was interesting. James was the scoutmaster who killed himself when Timothy was seventeen. Was that the fork in the road?

> **What are other ways now you can meet that same need?**
>
> **7/30/2009**
>
> **12:31 AM**

I don't know.

7/30/2009

12:32 AM

> **That would be something to give some thought to.**
>
> **7/30/2009**
>
> **12:33 AM**

I will as soon as I can start dealing with the problems and issues I've been avoiding.

7/30/2009

12:34 AM

That's going to take some effort and energy on your part because there have been some habits developed and reinforced over what sounds like a long time.

7/30/2009

12:37 AM

I know and I'm ready to deal with that.

7/30/2009

12:37 AM

You are a very hard worker in many other areas of your life - it's to take those skills now and apply them to being honest with yourself and your relationships and getting help.

7/30/2009

12:40 AM

Now that I can admit that I need help I think I can start taking the next steps to putting my life back together again and stop hurting all the people around me in the process.

7/30/2009

12:44 AM

Lisa is waiting on her STD results. Does she have reason to be concerned?

7/30/2009

12:47 AM

No. Thank god I can at least ease her mind in some way.

7/30/2009

12:48 AM

What makes you think she doesn't have to be worried?

7/30/2009

12:51 AM

Because Amanda is clear and I was never with anyone else.

7/30/2009

12:51 AM

I know that Las Vegas has 24-hour wedding chapels, but I was unaware that they had 24-hour STD clinics. How did he *know* that she was clear? I can't say that my mind was eased at all. Besides, I still believed that there had been a different woman at the house.

Time will tell.

7/30/2009

12:53 AM

I know but at least I know I didn't damn her with that on top of everything else.

7/30/2009

12:54 AM

I need to sign off. I'm wiped, it's been a horrendous 18 days and this is only the beginning. I 'll be watching for the two e-mails that you said you'd put together.

7/30/2009

1:01 AM

I'll start working on that soon. I need to try and rest too. Thank you for listening to me tonight.

7/30/2009

1:02 AM

We slept. The wine allowed me a fitful rest; I was up at dawn yet again pacing the grounds. My mom slept hard that night as the last few weeks caught up with her. We received another text from Timothy as we cleaned up our room that morning:

I'm working on cleaning up my legal obligations this morning in Iowa. Once I am on the road I will start putting together the information we went over last night.

7/30/2009

10:19 AM

okay

7/30/2009

10:20 AM

Thank you. I'm done avoiding this now and I will work to make this right. I need help and I can finally admit that.

7/30/2009

10:22 AM

The promised lists of debts and solutions never came.

Instead, we were greeted by a text stating that his lawyer told him to avoid further contact. How convenient.

Even after the arrest, he still was not aware that I had access to his junk mail account. For a brilliant man, he certainly had some lapses in intellect. He and Amanda were e-mailing while he sat in the backseat of his parent's van heading back to Atlanta the next day.

Hi Tim,
I appreciate the conversation we had earlier, as it reinforced the truth that this really did happen, and brought me out of the

little momentary fantasy I was in today in which I was pretending things were normal.

I really have to protect myself in this situation - I can be here for you, but I can't assume you can be trusted, as much as it feels good to act like we are okay. I appreciate you knocking me back into reality. It's ironic, isn't it, that you had to do that for me today?

But don't worry - I am still your friend, with the limitations I set out yesterday of course, and I am here if you need me. I like phone calls more than texts, as you already know. :) But the point is that you can contact me when you need anything, or just to say hi. I can offer you an ear, some encouragement, or a swift (rhetorical) slap in the face if I see that you are slipping into dangerous territory.

I don't trust you, and I will protect myself, as painful as it is to do so.
I hope your drive is going well...
Amanda

PhD candidate, Geography
Iowa State

Don't wait for strangers to remind you of your duty,
you have a conscience and a spirit for that.
All the good you do must come from your own initiative.
-Popul Vuh

Amanda,

Thank you for everything. I'm sitting down with an attorney at eleven and then leaving for Georgia shortly afterwards. I'll keep you in the loop and let you know how things go. It means more than anything to me right now to have you as a friend. I won't take advantage of your trust again.

Tim

Tim,

Good luck with everything, and don't hesitate to ask me for help or just an ear to listen.

Amanda
PhD candidate, Geography
Iowa State

Don't wait for strangers to remind you of your duty,
you have a conscience and a spirit for that.
All the good you do must come from your own initiative.

Amanda,

I'm taking each day one at a time now with my eyes open to the truth. I'm going to do whatever it takes to work through this and come out the other side clean. I'm meeting with an attorney this morning to try and stay out of jail and then heading to Atlanta to work on

trying to resolve things there. I know I've made terrible
mistakes but I'm done avoiding them.

Tim

His eyes closed again to the truth mere days later. He secured a
divorce attorney and immediately began to influence him with
fabrications. I guess he disregarded the following message from
Amanda:

On Jul 30, 2009, at 7:48 AM, Amanda wrote:

I just noticed how much the quote below is pertinent to your
personal situation and goals for change right now...

Don't wait for strangers to remind you of your duty,
you have a conscience and a spirit for that.
All the good you do must come from your own initiative.
-Popul Vuh

Sweetie, you're a bit slow on the uptake. My family has been
giggling over that line for weeks.

Even though he never took "responsibility" or worked to "make
things right," this text conversation was a gift. It allowed me to see the
suicide letter for what it was, a desperate attack from a man who was
cornered and panicked. It was no different than a trapped cat lashing
out with its claws. It was a last frenzied attempt to try to save his
"self," even as he acted to take his own life. He truly was a broken
man.

His work had evolved into creating three-dimensional models of trade show booths. He was especially known for his skill with lighting that made the renderings appear especially lifelike. His work with the shadows apparently extended to real life. He tried to hide in the shadows, but instead he became a shadow of himself.

I will never know for sure what sent him into the darkness, but I have some suspicions. He found himself unemployed for the second time in 2005 when his current employer shut down. He was not having much luck finding work, so he made the decision to invest in computers and expensive software so that he could teach himself how to do computer rendering and open his own company. I was nervous, but was willing to be supportive as he gave it a shot. As always, he impressed me with his ability to master a new skill quickly; he created images that rivaled those in magazines and movies within months. He took out an LLC and filed the other paperwork to start up a small business. He was still in touch with others in the industry, including former clients, and said that was going to be his conduit for jobs.

From what I knew, the company was relatively successful, bringing him back to close to his prior income level for the two years he ran it before again taking a job with a traditional employer.

Now, I have my doubts. I know he was working during that time; I saw drawings, e-mails, and even an award that made it into a trade magazine. What I didn't see were the actual checks from the clients. I now believe that his "income" during that period was largely subsidized with credit he took out and his retirement accounts. A manufactured salary, created from denial and desperation.

During that same period, he began to develop more expensive tastes. The Target shirts were replaced with Banana Republic. The brand new 4Runner took the place of an old truck. He always wanted the new gadget, and he soon armed himself with an iPhone, a Kindle, and a Cannondale bike. He usually claimed to get these from Ebay at a steep discount. I somehow doubt that now.

I think he was feeling ashamed of his lack of success and wanted to temper it by projecting the air of a prosperous man. This also coincides with when he cut off contact with his father. They were always in similar industries and spent all their time together "talking shop." I guess it became too difficult to talk shop when the shop in question was as mythical as the one at the North Pole.

I suspect that was the beginning of the hole he mentioned. Instead of admitting to himself that there was a hole, he began to work to cover it, subtly at first, but reaching a fevered pitch as time went on. I think he decided upon that course to hide the hole from me, but even more to hide it from himself, executing a self-inflicted lobotomy. I think he was afraid to look at that darkness head-on, so he diffused it as much as possible. For a time, the cover over the hole held. By March of 2009, however, the hole had become too large to hide and the camouflage was caving in, pulling me and his new wife in with the collapse.

He began to build a new identity as he distanced himself from the old. He had always gone by his full name, Timothy, partially to distance himself from his father, who went by Tim. My husband began to introduce himself as Tim around his 30th birthday. I found out later, in a conversation with his former employer and friend, that he created elaborate stories at work beginning in 2007 about himself and about me. While he remained loving and attentive at home and with our friends, he was demonizing me in the eyes of his coworkers. In World of Warcraft, he shifted from a character of the Alliance to one of the Horde, while in real life he was trying to play both sides at once.

He was always skilled at bending the truth to serve his needs, although it was usually done in humor or to open an otherwise closed door. I first saw this trait when we were sixteen on a trip to the mall. A pollster approached us and asked us to participate in some survey about cookie preference. Timothy glibly replied, "I can't. I'm diabetic."

The rapidity and deftness with which he delivered the falsehood shocked me, but I chose to ignore the warning sign. Later, he used exaggerations or fabrications like I used degrees to move his way up the ladder of professional success. He frequently claimed he knew how to do something, only to then scramble behind the scenes to make it true. His ability to lie did make me nervous, but, then again, I err too much on the other side of truthfulness. I trusted him not to use his skill in fabrication against me and I saw no harm in the applications that I witnessed. His years of practice served him well as he sought to weave new tales to hide his spending and create a new life, keeping all the storylines straight. He knew the exact proportion of truth to lie to make each falsehood believable. The deceptions held until the entropy of the closed system grew too great to contain.

I believe in all of this that he was deeply unhappy. He grew up in a family where emotion, much less depression, was not talked about. He saw his parents address their sadness and fear with alcohol and I believe he attempted the same. He hid his wounds like an injured dog crawling off into their den. He tried to handle his pain alone, and in doing so, only caused his wounds to fester.

His only cry, which went unrecognized and unheeded by me, was his favorite song those last few years: Johnny Cash's cover of

"Hurt," originally by Trent Reznor of the Nine Inch Nails. The song speaks of pain and emptiness, lies and letting down loved ones. I heard that song hundreds of times during my marriage, but I never really listened. Those lyrics echo the voice of my suffering husband, only recognized too late.

All big things have small beginnings; the seeds of his self-destruction were planted long ago and grew to great size while encapsulated in the darkness of his mind.

"Dear John" Letter Sixth Interpretation (July 29, 2009)

Lisa,

I'm afraid there is no easy way for me to say this – I'm leaving. *Apparently there is no easy way for you to do it, either.* We have had a long and rich life together but I can no longer live this life anymore. *Or any life?* As I told you several months ago, I feel as though we have been drifting apart for a number of years. *I think you have drifted away from yourself.* It was a gradual thing but I can honestly say that it has reached a point where I no longer can share time with you without wondering when I can be away from you again. *Again, I think you can't stand to be near yourself; you are running from who you have become. That never works.* I can't keep living this lie – it's not fair to either one of us. *It is interesting, then, that you left one life of lies for another. You were not at all truthful with Amanda.* I will continue to support you as best I can from wherever I end up. *Do you really believe this?* I will continue to work for DS but I would appreciate if you didn't involve them in this matter. *You're done with being able to segment your life; your choices have blown apart those walls.* We had some amazing times together and I will treasure these memories for the rest of my life. *I won't. You have taken them away from me.* I think people change as they experience life and unfortunately we have grown so far apart that I simply cannot relate to you in any way. *That is sad.* I know that this will hit you very hard and for that I am sincerely sorry. *I think you are. That night when you wailed, "I'm so sorry I failed you," rang true. I wish that could have stopped you years ago from inflicting so much pain.* I have never wanted to do anything to harm you in any way but in doing so I have made myself unhappy for many years. *Are you blaming me for your unhappiness? Not fair – you were never honest with me, never gave me a chance.* I know that once you recover from the shock of this you will bounce back and live a happy and satisfying life – a better and more honest life than I could ever hope to offer you. *I now notice that not only did you not claim that your life would be more honest, you also did not claim that your life would be happy or satisfying. Did you already realize that your path led to nowhere?* Everything I have left behind is yours and all I have taken is my clothing and the equipment I need to make a living. *You have taken so much more; nothing left is untainted by your deception and betrayal.*

I will never ask you for forgiveness or understanding. *You have been consistent with that. You do not ask me for forgiveness, but you continue to ask others for pity. I do not find you pitiful; I find you despicable. Someone who can be so cold and so cruel does not deserve sympathy.* I am a coward who couldn't tell you to your face that I am leaving. **You are a coward. I don't think you could even admit to yourself that you were leaving until it was inevitable.** If I don't do this now then I probably never will. **How would you have ended it?** I need my life to have some sort of meaning to it and unfortunately working in the basement of my house and watching tv and playing video games isn't it. **Where do you expect to find meaning?**

I'm sorry but my life is very quickly becoming that of my parents. **Are you referring to the excessive drinking?** No matter how much I see that, it feels like there is nothing I can do to change the path that I am on. **You do not seem to be trying too hard to change your path.** From this point on there is nothing more that I can say other than how sorry I am for leaving you in this way. **I'm sorry too.** I will do everything I can from this point forward to try and make this as easy on you as possible. **Did you need to tell yourself this to alleviate some guilt?** I didn't strip the account to leave. **So why did you strip the accounts? Where did all the money go? What purchases did you make to try to buy happiness?** I sold everything downstairs that I felt was part of the old me that I so desperately need to leave behind. **You cannot run from yourself; you will always catch up.**

Lessons From the End of a Marriage

Lesson Eight

It is okay to not have all the answers.

I was always a good student. I took advanced classes, did all my homework, and studied for tests. I expected perfection from myself. If I made a 100 on an assignment, and I could have made a 102, I would berate myself for days. I was that kid in class that you hated; you know, the one that had her hand up to answer every question. I was used to having all the answers or, with a trip to the library, being able to find the solutions. Once Timothy left, I realized how little I knew.

August 2009

After returning from Iowa, I had to shift back into my role as a teacher. I lived a split existence: I taught math to unsuspecting students while awaiting phone calls from the District Attorney's office in Iowa for news on the felony bigamy case. I composed e-mails to parents between e-mails to the local police. I went to the gym to escape while fielding calls from my divorce attorney. I was between two worlds, and I felt like an interloper in both.

On the first day of school with students, I awoke to a text message and missed call from Ben. He directed me to visit a website. Confused, wondering what this had to do with anything, I navigated to

225

the site while putting on my shoes for work. I was greeted with Timothy's mug shot and the headline:

Prosecutors Charge Georgia Man With Bigamy

Oh. My. God. It made the news. It was real. In print. This never crossed my mind. I envisioned that this would remain my own private hell until I was ready to reveal it.

There was the mug shot again, this time enlarged enough to really see. His eyes were empty, his skin pallid. He did not look like the Timothy I had known. He was not the Timothy I had known. My eyes scanned the image, looking for familiarity. There was none.

The article stated that he had left his wife with a text message and married an Iowa woman six days later. It mentioned that he was caught because his wife found evidence in his e-mail account. They failed to mention that he held me and kissed me two weeks before his wedding. It didn't tell the story of the depths of his lies and betrayal. The article neglected to describe me, a shattered shell of myself, as I attempted to navigate the twisted funhouse mirrors of my new life. But at least they got the facts right.

I printed the article before I left for work. I kept it in my lap on my drive to the school, checking it at every red light. It was another tangible sign of the reality of it all. I almost hoped I would look down to find that the paper had disappeared, that it was simply a mental manifestation. The paper was immune to my wishes. It persisted.

Upon my arrival at work, almost two hours before the students were to arrive, it became clear that my mind was not ready to focus on school tasks. I pulled up the article again, rereading the comments left by readers.

On a whim, I entered" Timothy Black bigamy" into Google. He was the first five hits. Not only had Ames, IA picked up the story, but the local news in Atlanta was reporting as well. I settled in to read the comments posted by my fellow Atlantans.

The responses made me laugh and made me angry at the same time. It was evident that this was way out of anyone's frame of reference. I know that prior to July, I thought of the Showtime series "Big Love" whenever bigamy was mentioned. People did not seem to understand that Timothy did not want two wives, he simply wanted a new one without having to face the first.

That evening at the gym, his face splashed across the televisions while I was on the treadmill. My phone began to ring with requests for interviews. I had to notify my principal of the situation in case the reporters tracked me to my school. Timothy's actions refused to let me rest.

Timothy began to receive intensive counseling services while he stayed with his parents in Atlanta. I was privy to this information because he was still on my health insurance (complete with the higher family premiums that I was required to pay until the legal divorce) and so I received all of the statements on my account. Along with the bills for his ambulance ride and ICU stay, I received charges for a full-day outpatient program. I wondered if he was sincere in his therapy or if it was a ploy to manipulate the Iowa courts in his favor. I hoped he was receiving help; he certainly needed it.

His first court appearance in Iowa for the bigamy charge coincided with open house night at school. I ducked out early to call the prosecutor. I learned that he did show up to court and he did have an attorney present. He was officially charged with felony bigamy and a court date was set for later that fall. His computers and passport were returned to him. He would waste no time putting the latter to good use.

He returned to Atlanta with his parents and secured a divorce attorney. He immediately went on the offensive, claiming that I was acting inappropriately by reporting his criminal activities to the police. I was a bit confused, as I always thought that it was illegal to be aware of a crime and *not* report it. His lawyer was all too happy to take part in the attacks, painting me as a vindictive woman set out to destroy her hapless husband.

They requested that the 4Runner be returned to Timothy. Up until this point, the vehicle had been stored in the garage in our old home. I ran the car twice a week to ensure that it remained in good condition, but I wanted nothing else to do with it. I agreed to hand the car over as long as he took over the payments, as my name was also on the account. The plan was for me to place the vehicle in the driveway and have Timothy obtain the keys from my lawyer.

I carefully backed the car out, turned off the engine, and sat in the driver's seat looking around. I had removed all of his personal belongings from the car when we had returned from Iowa. I went back inside the house and took a few items from the kitchen island to put back in his car. I placed a pocket watch from his deceased grandfather on the seat along with a cassette tape made by his childhood's best friend's father, who was a folk musician. Tears dropped on the gifts as I said goodbye yet again.

I locked the car doors, sealing his past within. I kept the rumpled papers that contained his wedding vows.

I received a call from the paralegal that worked for my attorney the next day; she was disgusted that my husband was flirting with her when he picked up the keys. Maybe he was on the prowl for wife number three?

October 2009

The weeds grew taller with every trip to the marital house, a sign of passing time and the decay of my former life. It was as though the house represented the entirety of our marriage, so carefully and lovingly built and tended, only to be abandoned and neglected. Every glimpse of the home was a reminder of the finality of the situation. By October, I could no longer stand to see the house. I never went back.

I was hopeful about the felony trial. I was preoccupied with his having to face some sort of legal consequence for his actions. I wanted him to have to try to move forward with the label of "felon" affixed to his record with permanent glue. My visions of long prison sentences had been replaced with the more realistic images of a short probation. I never imagined he would walk away unscathed.

Before the case even went to trial, the judge elected to grant him a diversion, a special "out" that can be offered to first time criminals charged with non-violent crimes. As long as he met the conditions of the diversion, which included protracted counseling and substance abuse support, as well as an apology letter to his two wives, he would be able to move forward with a clean record. If he failed to fulfill the orders, he was supposed to immediately and automatically be charged with the felony.

He has never met those conditions, unless he attempted to send my apology by carrier pigeon, but has escaped the felony. While I was faced with the repercussions of his actions, he received a "Get Out of Jail Free" card and the confirmation that he could continue to con.

His confidence built, he showed no boundaries in the divorce proceedings. My maternal grandmother had started an account for me when I was a child that was to be used for my education. By the time we moved to Atlanta, there was $20,000 in the account. We elected to use that as a down payment on the house, since mortgage interest rates at the time were double that of student loans. That fall, I received communication through the layers of lawyers that Timothy was claiming that money as his and was demanding that I pay it to him. After an exhaustive search of old tax records, my mom found the needed evidence. A quick scan and e-mail of the check from the account in my name shut down Timothy's latest claim.

He claimed we had not been intimate in over a year. I guess he had conveniently forgotten about July 4, 2009. Twice. He claimed we had been separated for two years, but continued to live in the same house. I guess that explains the number of texts he sent that said he loved me within the period in question. In all of this, he never did mention his earlier assertion that I had been married to Mark (Marc?) Mercer for the last several years. I guess that story had been abandoned. Poor Mark (Marc?).

He claimed in the discovery documents that he had not been hospitalized within the past year. I wonder how he would explain away the daily bills I received from his ICU stay after his suicide attempt?

Timothy was undeterred. He wanted my teacher retirement. He wanted me to cover court costs and lawyer fees. He claimed I owed him. He disclosed nothing, his discovery documents sparsely filling a scant four pages (and only coming under threat of contempt) while mine emptied my printer of ink.

I felt confused. A stranger to the legal system, I had thought that it was there to protect my rights, to find and punish criminals. I was having to face the cold reality that, even though I was not given a chance to fight for my marriage, I was going to have to fight for myself. I realized the courts and their representatives are not equipped to deal with situations like this where the defendant was Dolus, the Greek god of deception.

There is so much about the legal process of divorce that is just not fair. A spouse can choose to be dishonest and actively hide information. I am disgusted by the fact that actions that would be deemed illegal against a stranger are allowed against a spouse. It is not unlike the way it was (and still is in some cultures) where a husband could forcefully take his wife without it being termed rape because of the legal contract between them. Why is it that a marriage contract makes despicable behavior tolerable in the eyes of the law? Why is it that just because I called him " husband," he could embezzle my money, steal my files, and abandon joint responsibilities without more than a slight slap on the wrist? If someone came into my home and did the same, they would be sitting in a jail cell, learning how to do pull-ups on a bunk bed.

I propose we need a new law: marital treason, the act of betraying one's marriage (there used to be a similar law called petty treason). This would include adultery, deception (financial and otherwise), and acting in a way that is in opposition to a marriage. Once convicted, the treasonous spouse would be required to pay restitution (enforced by payroll deduction) and forced to serve community service in a cause chosen by the spouse. For those, like mine, who like to run, their passports would be confiscated until the requirements of their conviction had been met. It seems as though the only time the law takes divorce seriously is in the case of child support (don't get me wrong here, I strongly support hunting down deadbeat parents). I'm not whining for alimony or excess; I just want what was stolen from me. The marital treason law would seek to identify and hold responsible those who chose to betray their marriage through deception. It's only fair.

The end of my marriage left me in a strange place. I was an active participant in a marriage that had an undetected cancer. Since my husband chose to disappear with a text message, I was left without the body upon which to perform a postmortem examination. Just like it is difficult to come to terms with an unexpected death until the underlying conditions are known, I found it almost impossible to accept the demise of my marriage without knowing what tore it apart.

I may not have access to the body, but I have access to sixteen years of history. History that contains clues to what might have precipitated and supported the malignancy that destroyed the marriage.

I could try to recreate him, a Frankenstein's monster made of collected memories and mementos from a life left behind. An amalgam whose sole purpose for existence would be a trip to the therapist's couch. I spent months with such a singular purpose, convinced that I could not move forward without some understanding of what made him tick.

I wanted a label that I could affix to him, "He is...that." There was comfort in the thought of a classification that would help to bring clarity to the utter confusion I felt just as I was accustomed to using the symbols of algebra to simplify mathematical scenarios. I sought to distill 16 years of actions with a single word. I looked to the label as an emulsifier, uniting the oil and vinegar of his two selves, since I could not reconcile them myself.

I used my extensive background in psychology, primed by combing through my mother's books when I was child and cultivated through hours of classes in college, to attempt to diagnose him. My initial reaction was that he was a sociopath, his cold heart hidden behind a mask of a loving spouse who used his veneer of normalcy to manipulate others for his gain. A sociopath has no empathy, no capacity for emotional depth yet they are incredibly skilled at speaking the words of love like a spider weaving a web to entrap its next victim. Like Leonardo DiCaprio's character in *Catch Me if You Can,* a sociopath views others solely as pawns in their game.

I found some comfort in that label of sociopath. It was absolute, leaving no room for nuance and, perhaps most importantly, it allowed me to justify not having any compassion or understanding for him, emotions I could not seem to rally after I viewed that text. I read books and blogs, condensing other's stories into traits and signs. Some aspects of the label certainly fit. He was intelligent and charming and had revealed great skill at spinning methodical lies. This painted him as a Gollum, an edifice that is hollow inside and unaffected by the flames within which he dwells.

I found some consolation, but the designation also meant that the entire relationship was a scam, a long con that extended back into childhood. It would mean that his first, "I love you," in German, was uttered as a manipulation. The label indicated that his tears as he recited his wedding vows merely spilled to give the illusion of emotion and the sobs that shook the bed 10 years later were false. Not only did I not want to believe that; I couldn't believe that. He had shown the capacity for empathy for me, and for others. He displayed true emotions. He did not have the early behavior problems or impulsivity that normally accompany a diagnosis of sociopathy. His skill at manipulation and deception was astonishing, but his was a monster that was created, not born.

Additionally, sociopaths feel no guilt. No remorse. They can destroy others as easily as a ravenous person can tear into a meal. Although I did not trust his apologies in his texts to my mother, I did not believe that he was capable of cruelty without self-reproach. He may have buried his guilt deep, determined not to feel it, but his body betrayed him as he betrayed me. As his lies began to take over in 2007, his blood pressure rose to dangerous levels. He was on medication by 2008, yet the drugs failed to correct his stage two hypertension. Within another year, his pressures had crept even higher and he was at risk for a stroke at any moment.

He was scared. I know that was true. He complained of dizziness and nausea; I am unsure if those were genuine symptoms or ones simply fabricated for my sympathy. But I know he was frightened. I could see it in his eyes when he used his home blood pressure monitor. I could hear it in his voice when he described losing consciousness. I wonder if he ever saw a connection between his deceptions and his hypertension? Did he know when he took the sleeping pills in an effort to end his life that they would cause his blood pressure to surge? No matter how much he tried to hide the truth, his body wouldn't let it rest.

As I searched for answers, I was continually drawn to the fact that in retrospect he began to view others as his playthings, only puppets to be manipulated in the grand play he was choreographing. Was this a sign of narcissism? Unlike sociopaths, narcissists are deeply unhappy and seek to validate themselves through exaggeration and projection. They lie until it becomes a reflex, and they often fall sway to their own false stories all in a quest to avoid what causes them pain. Was he Icarus, blindly ignoring the warning signs that signaled his demise while he was enraptured by his own quest for glory? Yet again, it seemed as though this pathology would have shown itself long before the detonation of the marriage, but it never did.

On my journey for enlightenment, I next settled upon the diagnosis of addiction. Unlike the personality disorders of sociopathy or narcissism, addiction could manifest later in life. I saw signs of drinking when he was in Brazil and he admitted as much in his text conversation with my mother. Alcoholism ran in his family, so it was always something I kept an eye on. From what I was privy to, he had a normal relationship with alcohol; I only saw him drunk a handful of times in 16 years, and two beers with dinner was his norm.

Was he concealing an addiction to drugs? That could explain the missing money. Yet, he never seemed twitchy or nervous, never had behavior swings, and didn't shy away from blood or urine tests as the doctors sought to solve the riddle of his hypertension.

Gambling, then? Perhaps. I had seen him put a dollar in a slot machine once. Regardless of the vice, all addicts are experts at rationalizing their behaviors and they begin by convincing themselves. Addicts will certainly lie to protect their habits, but can an addict weave such masterful tales without getting the strands confused and twisted?

Maybe the answer could not be found in the *Diagnostic and Statistical Manual of Mental Disorders*. Possibly Jung had it right with his talk of a shadow self, the darker part of the self that resides in each of us that becomes more powerful when it is denied. It could be that after years of struggling to keep the shadow hidden in the depths, the pressure grew too much and the darkness took over, bringing chaos with it. This certainly explains his two personas and his two lives.

Or, maybe Socrates was on the money when he claimed that no man intends to harm another since that would only serve to harm himself. Rather, he proposed that immoral deeds were executed out of ignorance or to relieve suffering in oneself. Rather than approach any pain or shame that he was feeling, perhaps Timothy acted out with money and deceptions, each move serving to distract and sooth part of his wounded core.

Perhaps it was a mistake to think of him as all or none: sociopath or saint, narcissist or altruist, addict or ascetic, shadow or light, ignorant or enlightened. After all, he was ultimately just a man. I man I met and fell in love with when he was but a boy, still emerging from a vandalized childhood. He was my husband. My best friend. My lover. My partner. I realized I could spend a lifetime studying Timothy, trying to decode his mental processes, and still be no closer to the truth. Besides, I didn't want a degree in Timothy, which would be a diploma in B.S., of course.

Like Dr. Frankenstein's work, reconstructing his psyche was a fruitless endeavor. A task that distracted and that could lead to no ultimate good. So, ultimately, I had to choose to let go of the task before it gained a life that threatened my own. Rather than concern myself with labeling him, I needed to find understanding in myself. I am not Anubis; I am not tasked with determining his worthiness in the afterlife.

I may not have both bodies from the marital demise, but I had mine that could still be examined. He may have provided the initial malprogrammed cells, but I provided the medium that allowed them to grow unrestricted.

With time providing some insulation, I reread the "Last Con" letter, this time adding my voice to his outrageous claims. The letter and his actions upon his return to Atlanta made me angry all over again.

By the time you get this I expect I will already be gone for good. ***Did you really expect this, or were you being manipulative? You let others know of your plans, but you did not reveal your location.*** I guess I just need somebody I can open up to right now before I close this final chapter for ever. ***Why my mom? You've avoided her for a while now.*** First and most importantly - my feeble defense. ***At least you recognize its flimsiness.*** Lisa is not the easiest person to live with (but hey! neither was I***!). I actually thought we did well living together. However, in retrospect, you were certainly difficult and I'm sure balancing your lies made being around me difficult as well.*** I lived a life with a woman who saw everyday as another problem***. What woman is this? I have never viewed every day as a problem and I view every problem as a challenge. I am well aware of my faults – impatience, intolerance, frustration – why didn't he attack me on those?*** Can you imagine living a life with a person with whom day in and out saw life as misery and seemed to desperately need for me to feel the same way. ***I tried to get help for you in May. How is that wanting you to be miserable? I took the initiative to hundreds*** *of examples of why I loved you.* This has been going on for many, many years. *Sixteen? Since you started taking money? When?* Ever since Lisa self diagnosed herself with shingles she has been suffering from colds, illness, aches, stress and a cadre of other problems that she just tells me I can't understand. *1) I had to self diagnose because the doctor was an idiot 2) I have always had health issues and you knew that from the beginning 3) I have never told you that you can't understand. And, just for the record, I've hardly been sick at all since eliminating the gluten you malign.* For years I have been sharing my life with a woman that only seems to be happy when she's letting you know just how miserable she is. *I'm sorry that writing down all of the things I loved about you came across as venting my misery.* For years I worked every hour of overtime and took on every job I could so she could have the freedom to try and find whatever might bring her some shred of happiness. *You don't get overtime. The financial records indicate that much of the time when you were supposed to be working, you were actually shopping, at the bar, etc. Those activities were meant to bring me happiness?* I gave up my life to work like a machine so she could have everything she needed to be happy only to just be reminded how unhappy and awful life is. *The life you created for yourself (and, in retrospect, me) was certainly awful and unhappy.* When I broke down to Lisa a few months ago she asked me if I might be depressed - ha! ***Then why did you tell me that you were not depressed?*** I've been depressed and contemplating suicide for years! ***So why is this the first I've heard of it? You looked at me like I was nuts when I asked you in May if I needed to worry about you hurting yourself.*** You would think that years spent sleeping in different rooms would have been some indication. ***Uhmm...I had to sleep in a different room a couple nights a week because you carried 50 extra pounds for a year that made you snore like a tractor. I returned to the bedroom as soon as the weight came off. I also resent that this line makes it sound as if there was no intimacy between us; we had an active sex life up until the day before I left for Seattle.***

I hope this is coming across so that this makes some sense. ***Nope.*** I have lost everything. ***Join the club.*** Yes I am guilty of leaving Lisa in the worst way possible and yes I am a coward but I didn't create the mess that she will unfortunately have to work with on her own. ***You didn't? You didn't open up credit cards in your name and hide them from me while you maxed them out? You didn't spend tens of thousands on Amanda? You didn't commit bigamy? I'm confused.*** Did you know that your daughter isn't the world's most responsible spender? ***This is*** *a funny line to all those who know me. For those who don't, enjoy these contrasts: Kindle (him) vs. active library account (me), 2005 4Runner (him) vs. 1999 Integra (me), 2nd generation iPhone (him) vs. ancient Sony flip phone (me). Get the picture?* This isn't entirely her fault as I should have just cut up the credit cards and screamed "NO MORE!!". *Yes, you should have cut them up – just not because of me. It is nice for him to accept some fault here.* I always just thought that if my bonuses kept coming I might be able to keep up with the tremendous amount of money we were throwing out the door each month. *Getting confused with those pronouns, honey. It is "I," not "we." The tremendous amount of money "I" was throwing out the door each month.*

I think things truly came to a head for me when Lisa self diagnosed herself with Celiac. *Maybe you want to have the colon biopsy for me? I'll be happy to schedule the appointment. Besides, I never claimed celiac, only gluten intolerance.*

Suddenly our $80 grocery bill jumped to a staggering $250 in which I was buying cheap seltzer water and bargain rate prepackaged sliced turkey. *...and dinners out several times a week. Our grocery bill increased, but nothing like that. And my restaurant expenditures all but disappeared.* I have never been able to say no to Lisa. *Not quite – you gave me limits all the time. We both said* *no to each other.* When she had to have a giant deck and an enormous hot tub I eventually gave in. *You mean the deck and hot tub we had planned since we purchased the house nine years earlier? The hot tub I worked summer school to pay for? The deck that I picked up extra tutoring sessions to help fund? Too bad I only had a year to enjoy it before you pulled this nonsense. And now I know I worked those hours to help fund your depravity.* When she had to have thousands of dollars in deck furniture I gave in to the pressure. *We both couldn't wait for the spring shipment of outdoor furniture to hit the stores.* When everything was done with the deck and suddenly she was under more pressure and had to go on vacation even though she promised me the deck would be the end of the spending spree. *What? You suggested and booked the trip.* I eventually just caved and gave in. *Gave in to what? The desire to run away?* Look at the pictures on my laptop - do I really look happy? *No thanks – I don't want to look at your pictures.* I would send you the pictures but I have nothing but the clothes I'm wearing and my phone. *...and the brand new super-expensive bike and the digital camera I had never seen and...* Please let Lisa know that the password to my laptop is mondoabo42 and the password to the DS computer is monkeybone. *Why? The last thing I want to do is traipse around in the debris of your lies.*

The DS computer is just that - a work machine. **And now it is in the possession of the police.** My laptop is whatever she wants. **Do you think I actually want your machine?** It holds the scraps of what was my life and I hope she smashes it into tiny little pieces because that machine brought me more happiness than I have felt in a great many years. **That machine allowed you to con – is that where your happiness came from?** I had thought today that I would be able to take my equipment and the DS gear pack it into my car and move to Michigan to try and save my job**. Ben told you that it would become more difficult if you continued to lie. And yet you lied.** As Lisa has seen fit to tell the police to take everything from me then even that little shred of hope is even gone. **Again, did you expect me to simply turn a blind eye as you fucked me over? Not likely. I'm sure that you're familiar with the saying, "Hell hath no fury like a woman scorned."** I meant what I said in my letter - I would have worked for the rest of my life to help Lisa to pay off OUR debt. **Is that why the uncontrolled spending continued in Iowa and you refused to contact me? That doesn't exactly seem like someone trying to make things right.** I want to be completely clear in this matter as my arresting officer asked a question that could only have come from one place. **What does that mean? Do you even know that I'm the one who initiated the investigation and built the case?** I didn't steal and hide anything. ***Excuse me?*** I didn't empty out our account and hide the funds someplace else. ***I have no doubt that there is no hidden money. You appear to be unable to hold on to the smallest fortune. As to what has become of the money, I will most likely never know.*** To do what I have done I cashed in my retirement funds to try and live this little dream. ***You cashed those in months before you left to continue your nightmare. That money is long gone.*** I knew it would come to an unpleasant ending but I had hoped that everybody wouldn't turn against me. ***So you did know that you couldn't continue your con forever? Why are you surprised that people turned against you? Do you think that you can be an ass and still be adored? Not likely.*** It's ironic that I would turn to you to share my tale as your daughter has done nothing but complain about you but you can think of this as my final confession - my last rights. ***That is a low blow. I have had a strained relationship with my mom at times, but I certainly do not do nothing but complain about her. You knew that would make her doubt me and pierce her deeply. You ass.*** You somehow seemed to be the right person to share with. ***And Amanda, too?***

I would like to share my love and time with Amanda. ***Oops, I guess you messed that up by marrying her.*** Christ....

How do I explain myself. *I don't think you can explain yourself.* Yes. I love her. *I don't think you are capable of love.* Yes I have given up everything for this amazing woman. *True.* Yes. I am damned all the more for it. *True.* I met the amazing woman in Las Vegas while I was working a show in March. *True again. Three in a row – I'm impressed.* I was feeling especially low after an awful night spent pretending to enjoy the company of people who cared for nothing but themselves. *Interesting comment; I do believe that you are more self-centered than any of them.*

To be honest - I was looking for an end that night. *There you go again with that "honest" word. I'm sorry, but I can't believe a thing you say. You're track record isn't exactly clean.*

Instead after walking for a few hours I stepped into a little bar to listen to a bit of music and met the last bit of happiness of my life. *You mean you met a nice and naïve girl that would believe your bullshit.* She just seemed to glow to me from across the room. *What is this, a romance novel?* Maybe it was her smile or her eyes -hell it was probably both that both drew me to her and scared me half to death. *I just keep reminding myself that he sent this to Amanda; the flattery was intended for her.* I kept trying to work up the courage to leave when I looked across the room and found her right in front of me. *Yeah, courage isn't something you seem to have in droves.* All thoughts of flight left my mind at that moment and I was suddenly desperate to talk to this amazing woman. *Wait? All thoughts of flight left your mind? Then why did you make plans to go to Uganda?* Let me be clear at this point *Good, because you have not been clear about anything yet.* - I have been on the road for a very, very long time and have spoken to many women of the course of my travels. *Likely.* Never have I ever cheated. *And, why should I believe you now? Besides, even if you technically had not cheated, you had been lying and covering up your actions for years. Betrayal comes in many forms and not all of them have breasts.* As these are my final words I can and will say and tell whatever I want and damn the world if you don't believe me. *You have been saying AND doing whatever you want for years. I wouldn't expect you to stop now.* This woman was different. *Right place. Right time. Right plans for a trip to Africa.* I wish I could explain to you why my dear reader but there was something magical about her. *"My dear reader?" What the hell?* I met this woman in the sinkhole that is Vegas only to learn that she understood my stupid sense of humor and enjoyed my company. *...and believed your lies.* Even more importantly she was vastly smarter than me and didn't rub it in my face. *More educated? Yes. Better grammar? Absolutely. More developed moral character? Without a doubt.*

But smarter? I'm not too sure about that one. I wish you could meet her - she is without a doubt the most incredible and intensely amazing person I have ever met in all of my travels and somebody I am proud to have shared my final moments with. ***I'm sure she appreciates this line.*** My relationship with her was the best and happiest I have been in..... it was the happiest I have ever been and now it's over. ***The happiest you've ever been? In a three-month long distance relationship based completely upon lies. That's sad.*** I wish that I could have some closure with her before I have to do this awful thing to myself. ***Before you "have" to do this awful thing to yourself? It sounds like you're not taking responsibility for this action either.*** I wish to everything that is good and right in the world that she didn't turn her back on me the way she did. ***What did you expect? Did you think she would never find out?*** I gave up everything and now I am left by myself with just this one awful answer to all of my problems. ***You gave up everything? That sounds rather martyr-ish of you. More like you destroyed everything.*** I love Amanda because she gave me the only hope and happiness I have had in too many years. ***Uganda?*** I love her because she let me be myself. ***Okay, now that is just too funny. She didn't know ANYTHING about the real you.*** Now I end my life because in the end we simple die alone with nobody to care. ***No, we don't all die alone. You pushed everyone away.***

I would have sent this tonight but the razor in my room wasn't up to the job of finishing this nasty task. *More likely you weren't up to the task of using the razor.* I will send this all later this morning as soon as I can secure the proper tools to end my life. *"Proper tools"? That sounds a bit melodramatic.* I didn't want this but I am left alone and hopeless. *Not left. You put yourself there.* The only people I have ever cared about in my life all want me dead - at least I can bring them some comfort by making this happen. *The only people you ever cared about? Do you mean yourself? It does sounds like you want yourself dead.*

I'm sorry for unloading this on you but I needed to share with somebody before I left for the eternal darkness. *Again with the drama. I know you used to dream about being a writer, but this is a strange platform.* I know what waits for me after this life - nothing. Eternal and everlasting emptiness. *Sounds like you've already found emptiness without the dying part.* Who knows - maybe some scrap of me still lingers on afterwards to ponder life's greatest questions or maybe I will wind up in a world of eternal hell and damnation. *Is there any scrap of you left now? Or have you already been swallowed up by the darkness? If you do end up in hell, at least you've studied "Dante's Inferno" so you know what you're in for.* But then really - who cares what happens to me. *Before*

July 11, I would have taken a bullet for you. Now? I'll buy the bullet for you. I will die alone. We all die alone.

Be well Cathy. *Be well? Now that I've destroyed your daughter and told you that she always complained about you...be well?* I'm sorry for emptying my soul to you but I had no place else to turn. *That is what happens when you lead a life of dishonesty.* Please help Lisa through these hard times and never tell her of this letter. *Even if it will bring me "closure" as you stated earlier? That's sick.* If you ever have a chance to meet Amanda I know you understand just how amazing she really is and how crushed I am to lose her. *I'm sure my mom can't wait to meet her.* I can't live without her and she thinks of me only as a monster. *Maybe because you are?* Was I really so wrong to want to try and find happiness in my life? *Wrong to look for your own happiness? No. Wrong to destroy everything in your path like King Kong on a rampage? Yes.* I guess the final answer is yes.

May you live in peace. *Peace has been a rare commodity since you left.* Please forget me - I was never worth anything anyway. *It's a little hard to forget 16 years and such a dramatic ending. As to your worth, it has certainly diminished.*

In the end I know that nobody ever really cared about me - they just cared about what I could do for them. *I loved you more than you will ever understand. I would have done anything for you.* I just wish I could have done something for myself over the years to try and find true happiness. *I wish you could have asked for help. I wish you could have been honest with me and with yourself.*

Tim

Lesson Nine

Your worth is not tied to your to-do list.

The biggest insult that could have ever been directed my way is that I was lazy. That label sent me into a panic, frantically searching for more scraps of paper upon which to compose even more to-do lists. I organized my life by bulleted lists, a series of tasks to be accomplished and crossed out only to move on to the next one. I hopscotched through each day from item to item, and never paused between. The space between was an uncomfortable void, a chasm with no definable goal and no clear direction. An interval to be avoided at all costs.

My self-worth was always tied to my lists. More marked-through tasks meant that I was a better teacher. A better wife. A better person. It was clear and definable: do this, accomplish that, and you will feel good about yourself while avoiding the fear associated with any interludes.

I was always driven in all areas of my life. The good thing about being driven is that you get quite a few tasks accomplished. The down side of being driven is that you never really slow down to listen.

Fall 2009

Even my divorce became a series of items on a to-do list. I dutifully filled out each form requested by my attorneys, gathered and organized evidence, and crossed off tasks as I awaited the final and legal cross off of my marriage. I only halfway joked that I should be my own legal assistant.

My lists extended beyond the legal system; I even posted goals above my computer to guide my recovery:

Complete and publish a book about my story
Find job in the Northwest
Find place to live in the Northwest
Go on a date
Complete a half or a full marathon
Go on two weekend trips
Create a five-year financial plan
Volunteer at animal rescue
Make two new friends
Do two things that are out of character
Learn to cook one gluten-free meal to excellence
Laugh at least once each day

That list was my anchor, my guide. When I was lost, it instructed me in my next step. When I was hopeless, it provided me with optimism.

As is my nature, I wasted no time in working to cross accomplishments off my list. I began with running.

As a child, I was never athletic. I languished behind various complaints and never pushed myself physically. As I entered high school, I began to familiarize myself with the gym and I took up the sport of fencing. I learned to become comfortable with the discomfort and I discovered the joy to be found in reaching physical goals. I wanted to share my newfound love with others, so I pursued my personal training credentials during my first semester in college.

Although I never really used my certification, fitness was firmly anchored in my life. I was never too far from a gym, whether through a membership or found in the spare bedroom. When my schedule became too busy to workout after school, I began to wake up at 3:30 a.m. to fit in my session prior to the craziness of the day.

Even though I embodied fitness in many ways, I was never a runner. In fact, on the arrival of my thirtieth birthday, I had never run a mile. On a whim, I decided to change that. I think I chose the hottest day on record in August in Atlanta to start my journey. I drove to a nearby park that had a half mile track around its perimeter. I made it halfway around.

Undeterred, I went back the next day, and the next, each time making it a little further before I quit. I was limited by my lungs. They were unused to exertion in the humid and pollen-filled air with their constant wheezing prompting me to sooth them with additional dosages of Albuterol on top of my six other daily medications for asthma. I kept my ears ignorant of my lungs' struggles by plugging them with headphones that delivered the encouraging beats of Korn and Metallica.

So slowly, it was not even readily apparent, I began to breathe easier. I no longer felt the tight band of constriction when I moved from a walk into a run. I could feel the air moving deeply into my lungs, powering my legs through longer and longer excursions. I stated my ever-changing goals to Timothy.

"I just want to be able to run three miles."

He laughed, "You won't stop there. I know you too well."

A few months later, "I want to be able to run five miles. Just five. What's the point of any more than that?"

With a knowing grin and pinch on the backside, "I told you. I knew you wouldn't be able to stop."

Over the next two years, the last two of my marriage, I became a runner. I bought the shoes. My husband bought me the iPod and the iFit along with clothes appropriate for running in the Atlanta heat. I explored several routes and continued to push my maximum distances and speed. I was always a solitary runner. Although I encouraged my husband to give it a try, he never ran alongside me.

After the marriage ended, I craved the therapy of the miles on the trails. I ached for the authentic exhaustion that always followed a run. I longed for the soothing motion of my feet hitting the pavement. I was so weakened by the sudden trauma that I had to begin again. The hour long runs were replaced with five-minute trips. The safety of the treadmill took over for the seclusion of the trails as I was unsure of my ability to stay upright under pressure.

I could barely walk that summer, yet I signed up for my first ever race, a half marathon, being held that fall. Step by step, I regained my earlier fitness and pushed it to new levels, running further and faster than I ever had as a Mrs., as though the ring itself had been weighing me down. By most accounts, my first race was a disaster: I was sick, it was cold and raining, and I had to walk most of mile 12. By my account, it was perfect. It was the first goal I crossed off the list above my computer. It was progress.

Fitness also helped me accomplish another of my goals. I had joined a gym just down the street from Sarah's house and it became part of my evening routine. I was still unaware of men, the blinders I had for the duration of my marriage still firmly anchored on my face. I would walk in, move to the back of the gym where they featured the free weights, and focus on my workout. My only words, "Excuse me? Can I work in?"

All that changed when I was approached by a tall, heavily-muscled man with intelligent blue eyes and a smooth head. He introduced himself as Christian and, after a brief conversation, asked me if I wanted to go out. I had to bite back my initial response, "I can't. I'm married." Even though I was still legally betrothed, I was single in the truest sense.

After some internal debate over that night, I agreed. Within moments of accepting the date, I realized that my blinders were off. There were men everywhere. It was exciting and intimidating. I was interested, yet I had no idea what to do. My 13-year-old self was back in full force- I was boy crazy and had no idea what to do about it.

It was apparent from the start that Christian and I had an attraction to one another. It was also apparent from the start that it was way too early for me to entertain the idea of any sort of relationship. Luckily, Christian and I were able to transfer that interest into a friendship that persists to this day. So, with one encounter, I was able to cross two additional items off my list: go on a date and make a new friend. I still needed to learn how to handle my new-found interest in the opposite sex apart from my husband. That lesson came later.

One entry on the list was designed to never be crossed off; it was a reminder to be present each day and to enjoy the gifts that each moment had to offer.

Laugh at least once each day.

I didn't always accomplish this, but it reminded me that happiness could be found even in the midst of tragedy and that I didn't have to wait until this was over in order to smile.

To-do lists have a way of encouraging you to live in the possibilities of the future rather than the reality of the present.

At some point into adulthood, my life had become a waiting room. I sat quietly in my semi-comfortable thinly padded chair, one of many placed in a neat little row, content to rifle through familiar magazines. I patiently waited my turn, allowing others to move ahead only voicing an occasional protest. I grew accustomed to the discomfort of holding a single position. No one ordered me into that waiting room. No one even asked me to have a seat. I went in and sat myself down on my own volition.

Like a nervous patient awaiting an important consultation with the doctor, I was so focused on what was to come, playing with the possibilities, that I was largely unaware of my current surroundings. With the multiple losses I had experienced as a teenager, I was well aware that tragedy could strike at any time. I sat in fear that the future would deliver devastating news. I operated on the assumption that if I waited patiently enough, the bad news would never come.

Meanwhile, life in that waiting room was passing me by while I had my head buried in an outdated issue of *McCall's*.

Eventually, my name was called and I received the news I had been most afraid of: my husband was gone. Waiting patiently and planning carefully had not offered any protection from devastation.

It was an important lesson to learn.

The lists and the loitering gave me the illusion of control. As long as I wrote it down and waited my turn like a good little girl, tragedy would be held at bay. The truth? By dutifully writing down and crossing off items, I could control my own behavior, but no one else's. And, even more importantly, I was busy listing instead of being busy living.

Lessons From the End of a Marriage

Lesson Ten

Spreadsheets Can be Useful Dating Tools

Winter 2009-2010

As the calendar provided some distance from the events of the prior summer, I began to realize how lucky I was. I had escaped being mummified and stuffed in a canopic jar within my husband's tomb.

I was lucky. I never spent time in a decaying marriage. The lies that destroyed the relationship protected me for its duration, keeping me cloaked in relative comfort.

I was lucky. I never had to wrestle with the question of should I stay or should I leave? That decision was made for me.

I was lucky. I never had the pain of hoping for or trying for reconciliation. You cannot reconcile with someone who has become a ghost in his own life.

I was lucky. We did not have children. I did not have to see the pain on their faces, nor engage in a battle for them through the courts.

I was lucky. I had a clean, sudden amputation of my life, my marriage. The trauma was near fatal, but I was left with a clean cut with the sound of the ____ guillotine's blade still ringing in my ears.

259

1992-1994

My high school dating experiences were a bit unique. It was just my mom and me at that point, and she felt compelled to use her knowledge as a marriage and family therapist to try to ensure that I had the best and safest dates possible. I realized what this meant when I asked to go out on my first *real* date in the fall of my freshman year.

"Mom, Jim from art class asked me if I wanted to go out this weekend. Can I?" I asked, relatively confident that she would answer in the affirmative.

"Oh my. He's older, right? Drives? I knew this was coming, but so soon?"

"Mom. Yes or no?" I interrupted her questions, knowing they would continue with no answer if I let them.

"I guess," timid acceptance in her voice, "But, he needs to come in and meet me first," she added.

"Sure," I responded with a grin as I danced off to my room to call Jim and convey the good news.

I wouldn't have been so light-hearted if I had known what was to come.

The evening in question arrived, and so did Jim in his beat-up Chevy Blazer with Jane's Addiction announcing his approach through huge speakers in the back of the truck. I glanced back at my mom on the sofa as I went to answer the door. She had a manila folder on her lap. I briefly pondered the purpose of the folder, but I was more excited about the prize behind door number one.

After the introductions, my mom got down to business. Literally. Out came the folder, and with it, questions about Jim's family, his background, and his values. She was in full-on counselor mode, taking notes and asking probing questions. I was mortified, but also curious. She was getting into details I never heard while we were in art class. Finally, she was done and I proceeded to learn how to get into a big Texas truck while wearing a short skirt, an important lesson when one begins dating in San Antonio in the 1990s.

By the time Timothy came around two years later, my mom had perfected the inquisition hidden behind the guise of a counselor. She had decided that a subjective evaluation was not sufficient; it was time to pull out the big guns: the Myers-Briggs Type Inventory (MBTI). Naturally, she had administered this personality assessment to me on multiple occasions by the time I was 16, so she had a handle on my results.

I usually scored as an Introvert-Intuitive-Thinking-Judgment type (INTJ). This meant that I was prone to perfectionism, had a good imagination, yet perceived the world as driven by logic and reason. I was dependable and responsible and hard on myself and others. Furthermore, my type was said to be self-sufficient and not very touchy-feely. I couldn't argue with any of those results.

My mom gave Timothy the assessment. He scored as an Extrovert-Intuitive-Feeling-Perceiving type (ENFP). My mom proceeded to give us the meaning behind the words. ENFP types are big picture thinkers with lots of charisma. They tend to be enthusiastic and ingenious and are able to pursue almost anything that interests them. They are quick with solutions and often rely on their ability to improvise.

Maybe my mom in counselor's clothing pulled out the wrong assessment for Timothy. We may have learned more if he had taken the MMPI, designed to identify personality disorders and mental illness.

Winter 2009-2010

The last time I had dated, I was dating boys. Now, I would be dating men. The thought was exciting and nerve-wracking all in one. I had really shut my mind to other men once Timothy and I were a couple. I only allowed myself to feel attracted to "safe" men like Brad Pitt; I figured he wasn't much of a threat to my marriage. My blinders had been removed that fall. I was now aware of men, but no closer to understanding them or knowing how to date.

I had been assuming I needed to wait until I was fully healed before I dove into the matchmaking world. By December, I realized that healing was going to be a process. A long one. And I was not willing to sit idly by as I waited for the wounds to fully mend. I decided, utilizing no collective wisdom on the matter, that the following needed to be true prior to dating after a major break-up: 1) you have to want to be healed, 2) you have to be actively moving forward on your healing process, 3) you need to be able to accept responsibility for your actions and your happiness, and 4) you should be at a point where the good (or even okay) days outweigh the bad. Conveniently, I met all of those conditions.

My routine in those days was pretty straightforward: I went to work, went to the gym, and then went home to Sarah's. Christian and I watched movies or went for coffee. On the weekends, I might go out with some friends or go on long solo hikes. None of these offered much in the way of opportunities for dating. I had already exhausted the options at the gym, everyone at work was partnered, and there were no prospects in my social group. I knew I needed to learn how to date and I knew I would have to extend my reach if was going to happen.

I turned to the internet, posting the following profile on Match. *I am a compilation of contradictions. I am the petite woman in pink lifting heavy weight at the gym. I love to go to action movies in heels and listen to classical music while on a run. I am an award winning math teacher who almost failed algebra II. I am a natural introvert who loves to be around friends. I appear to be reserved, yet I am actually quite open with my feelings. I abhor conventions; I choose to celebrate what makes me unique.*

I am an intense person. I have strong opinions that I am not afraid to share. I make quick decisions and always know what my goals are. I am generally a thinker, analyzing everything around me.

I am a naturally curious person; I love to gain new knowledge. I love new experiences. I enjoy being with people who can teach me something new.

I love to travel, although circumstances have kept me close to home. I hope to remedy that soon.

I believe that you can tell quite a bit about a person by their habits. One of my habits is perusing a selection of websites to catch up on the news, the latest research, and the latest fun. I visit the following sites daily: CNN, The Weather Channel, Mental Floss, New York Times (especially the science and health sections), and Slate Magazine.

I value honesty, intelligence, and wit. I am looking to find someone to talk with, laugh with, and with whom to share experiences. Let's meet for coffee and see if we're a match.

The profile was completed with pictures my stepfather took of me during a Christmas visit. He and my mom got a laugh that they were responsible for the pictures used to find me a date.

I went into online dating almost blind. I received one important piece of advice from my stepbrother, Mike, who had met his wife on Match. He recommended that I not waste too much time on phone or e-mail contact up front. This way, it was easier to make a clean break if there was not a connection after meeting in person. I was thankful for the advice; my natural inclination would have been to e-mail for months prior to an actual meeting. His suggestion kept the carpal tunnel at bay.

As soon as I returned home from visiting Texas for Christmas, I put his advice to the test. Repeatedly.

Having never read, *The Rules* or spent much time around single people, I really had little to   no preconceived ideas of how dating was supposed to work. This turned out to be a blessing.

I approached each encounter with curiosity. I was not looking for a partner; I was looking to learn about dating and myself while having some fun in the process. I figured there was a lesson in every date, regardless of if it was good or bad, exciting or dull. I approached each encounter with an open mind, an open heart, and an open story. I shared a brief version of my life, including the events of the last several months, and disclosed that I was planning on evacuating the Atlanta area at the end of the school year. As expected, these revelations sent some men packing, but others remained undaunted by the information. Or maybe they just wanted to see me wear heels to an action movie.

I figured the best way to learn any new skill, regardless if it is solving quadratic equations or dating, is through practice. My routine of the previous fall was altered that winter. Now, I packed a bag in the morning that would see me through an entire day. I went straight to the gym after work, where my slacks and heels would be exchanged for spandex and lifting gloves. After a workout where I tried to not get too sweaty, I would peel off the spandex and gloves and replace them with jeans and an additional application of mascara. I would have dates lined up for each night of the week and sometimes two each day on the weekends.

Part of this time was spent discovering my sexuality apart from Timothy. He was all I had ever known and I had to rediscover intimacy apart from him. That was only a factor in a few cases, for the most part, the dates were spent hiking and sledding, watching movies and eating dinner. And drinking coffee. Lots of coffee. To this day, I love to walk into a coffee shop on the weekend or in the evening and pick out

265

the couples on an initial internet-arranged date. It always makes me smile with fond memories.

I approached my date selection like I approach an evening with Netflix. If I go in looking for a particular title, I am invariably disappointed when the service fails to deliver. If, however, I proceed with an open mind and try an unfamiliar title, I just might find a new favorite. I branched out into new genres, dating engineers and artists, introverts and performers. I grew more tolerant of differences in opinions and backgrounds; I learned to respect intelligence in varying forms, and I acquired knowledge about careers, interests, and hobbies.

It was a wild ride of excitement and emotions. I was excited when I was stood up for the first time; I felt like I had been awarded admission to the dating club. I was apprehensive about seeing one man, who shared a last name and first initial with my husband. I listened to men discuss why they had never been married or what led to the demise of their marriages. I asked pointed questions, using their responses to build a library about relationships.

When I was finishing my bachelor's degree, I worked as a substitute teacher. I used that time to practice and hone the skills that I later applied successfully in my own classroom. As a substitute, I had the freedom to try new ideas or approaches without fear. If it didn't work, it didn't matter; I would move on to a new set of students the next day. I viewed dating the same way. This was my time to experiment and practice so that the knowledge and skills would be ready for a relationship down the road.

I worked on tuning my internal lie detector, looking for clues in speech or body language that my date was being dishonest. I learned to tell when a man was insecure beneath his cloak of choice. I learned how to be aware of and look for inconsistencies between words and actualities without crossing the line into snooping. All of these lessons were easier to learn when I had nothing to lose; there was no fear of mistakes only a desire to learn.

Now, other than pure endurance, I did encounter another dilemma with my months of Match Madness. Even with my teacher-memory for names, faces, and interests, I could not keep the dates straight. So, I did what any self-respecting math teacher would do: I made a spreadsheet. The names were listed along the side with categories for phone numbers, e-mails, dates and locations, employment and interests, as well as a cell for miscellaneous information. I dutifully maintained that spreadsheet for the three months that I kept my account active.

The spreadsheet was certainly a useful tool; it prevented me from embarrassing mistakes and helped me objectively select dates. It was a helpful tool, but, in retrospect, I was actually using it as a security blanket. It took these men, these people with real stories, real vulnerabilities, and real desires, and it transposed them into mere data points on a screen. I could not fall in love with a data point.

One of my best lessons that winter came from a man I dated steadily for several weeks. He was acutely aware of my tendency to use my analytical mind as a shield, as a way to keep from feeling too much or risking too much. He challenged me on it, in a way that no one ever had before. In fact, his standard greeting to me was, "How are you feeling?" rather than the standard, and often trite, "How are you doing?" He would not let me weasel out with a pat response, though trust me, I tried. He pushed me to look inward, to feel, and to communicate those emotions honestly. After a few steady weeks and an out-of-state weekend trip, he disappeared. He contacted me several months later, apologetic and regretful. He expressed that he ran away out of fear of becoming too invested before I moved. I understood. During that short period we were together, we each learned important lessons about being open and vulnerable.

I didn't fall in love that winter. I didn't learn to trust. I didn't open my heart and let down my guard. Despite all of that, it was a successful few months. I practiced and listened. I learned about relationships and the latest version of Excel. I gained confidence and hope that I would fall in love again. And, I met the man that would eventually prove me right.

Lesson Eleven

Don't let fear be your chauffer.

I've never been very good at going downhill.

I was bribed with banana splits to encourage me to learn how to ride a bike. I was ten. I still am not comfortable on a bike; the slightest decline inspires panic and usually results in a dismount and walk. I used to think I could roller blade when I lived in San Antonio. It turns out that San Antonio is flat. Really flat. As soon as I took my "skills" to other less elevation-challenged cities, I realized that I really had no skill at all. But I did have a really sore behind. When I drive my standard-transmission car on the downside of a hill, I inevitably downshift beyond what is necessary. Even while running (look ma, no wheels!), I power up the hills and slow down on the descent.

I'm not sure what it is about hills that causes me pause. I know I get panicky, afraid that the situation will get out of control. It seems like any slight miscalculation is amplified through momentum, the snowball gaining size as it tumbles down the slope. Perhaps I don't trust progress made that is not under my own power. Maybe I just need to learn to surrender to gravity.

In all of these situations, I have let fear be my chauffer, turning over the reigns and letting apprehension steer the way.

March 2010

Winter turned into spring, each young green shoot pushing through the soil bringing with them a sense of hope and life to come.

For eight months, I had lived with the actual legal divorce in the forefront of my mind. I saw it as the summit of my Kilimanjaro, sure that once I reached the peak, the vista would be spread before me and my path would be clear. I feared that welcome peak; however, it possessed jagged edges in the form of the possible physical manifestation of my husband as well as the unknown actions of the legal process.

I didn't know if I wanted Timothy there or not. I now feared this man I once loved. But even more, I feared how I would respond to him. Would I be overcome with grief, yet again curled in a ball on the floor while heaving sobs shook my frame? Would the anger overcome any decorum, providing the opportunity for me to launch myself at him in a physical and verbal attack, ensuring that I would be the one in the handcuffs this time? Or, would I still feel attracted to him, my biochemistry unaware of all that had transpired. Or, perhaps most strangely of all, maybe I wouldn't even recognize anything of the man I knew. Maybe he would become a stranger.

I figured all of this debating was wasted mental energy. I had continued to track his whereabouts as we progressed through the divorce process. His wife made this easy; apparently he had not trained her in the espionage techniques that he had mastered as a bigamist on the sly. She was involved, through her position at the university, in coffee production in third world countries. To support her work, she started a blog. A blog which featured my husband. I learned through her ramblings that they had been able to take their planned trip to Uganda, just a little later than expected. They were still there showering with monkeys according to her post, just days prior to the scheduled court appearance.

I notified my attorney, providing her with a copy of the blog post. She smiled and stated, "I wonder if his attorney knows?" She composed an e-mail, questioning if his client planned to make the court date, attached the webpage, and sent it with a grin. We were not very fond of his attorney and yet we knew he was unaware of how much Timothy had been manipulating him. The response was immediate: denial, but with a false bravado. He couldn't imagine how bizarre reality could be. I understood. I was in his shoes just months before.

The morning of the divorce arrived. My mom, who had flown in to be of support, and I gathered up files and talked though possible outcomes as we got ready. The bonus room once again looked like a horizontal file cabinet, as papers and folders were strewn about the room. The drive to the courthouse took us past my school. This was one time I would rather have been going in to work.

We parked and slowly made the long trek to the entrance of the building. I wasn't sure if this was my death march or my freedom walk. My arms were shaking so badly upon entering the building that I struggled to free my purse from my shoulder and place it on the belt to be x-rayed. Once clear of security, my mom made a request to locate a bathroom. We found one just off the lobby, separated by a curved wall for privacy. I sat numbly on a brown leather bench in the hallway while waiting for my mom. I don't think I have ever felt so alone in my life.

Reunited again, we moved back into the main lobby and scanned the signs to find our assigned courtroom. Finding our direction, we began to move purposefully down the large central hallway, people passing us on either side. Wait. Was that? We stopped, looked at each other.

"Was that him?" I asked, referring to a tall, very skinny man in glasses that had moved by us on the left.

"I think so," she replied, turning to look over her shoulder at his rapidly disappearing frame.

I'm not sure what surprised me more: the fact that he was there or the fact that I barely recognized my partner of 16 years.

We entered the courtroom where I was ushered to a table in the front and my mom was guided to the seats in the back where Timothy's father already sat. My attorneys arrived shortly, carrying large files of documents and evidence. I no longer felt alone. I had my team there.

Timothy entered the room and moved to the opposite table. I examined him. His hair was familiar, dark and short with a manicured Van Dyke surrounding familiar lips. He had lost a significant amount of weight; his body had returned to that of a gangly teenager upon which hung an unfamiliar and seemingly expensive pinstripe suit. His contacts had been substituted with glasses. I could not tell if they were his old pair or if they, too, had been replaced. As my eyes scanned him, looking deeply for signs of my husband, I began to cry. Soft tears. Steady tears. I kept my gaze on him. From what I could tell, he never looked at me.

The judge came in, a smart, sassy blond that projected a good energy. She questioned Timothy, asking him if his attorney was expected. Timothy, managing to look nervous for once, said that the lawyer should be there. Enjoying watching him squirm as I was safely nestled next to my attorneys, I turned to them, "I bet he never paid his lawyer." I found out later I was right.

After several awkward minutes where the judge busied herself with the administrative minutiae of the trial, his attorney finally came bursting through the door. His cockiness was confirmed when the first words out of his mouth were to compliment the judge's hair. Her pinched mouth indicated her disapproval. Oblivious, he continued his saunter to the table where he pulled out a thin manila file. If this judgment was to be made on file size alone, I would have been the clear victor.

The judge had already perused the documents that had been submitted to the courts. She inquired about mediation and was informed that it had not occurred because Timothy had failed to produce the necessary documentation.

"It seems as though we have a bit of an unusual situation here. I would like to speak to the counsel in my chambers first."

All three attorneys moved through the door at the back of the courtroom, leaving me to gaze upon the effigy of my husband. He sat rigid, his eyes fixed straight ahead.

The lawyers returned, reconvening at their respective tables. Mine appeared almost jovial. His looked chagrined.

I learned the reason for the humor in my attorney's eyes as she later shared the judge's response to the synopsis of the tale. Turning to Timothy's attorney, the judge asked about his client, "What is he? Psycho?" Apparently his lawyer couldn't answer that question as he simply shrugged his shoulders in response.

We never did take the stand. All of the negotiations were done between the lawyers, us individually, and the judge. Essentially, everything worked out the way I expected. On paper at least.

I got my car; he got his. I got to keep my retirement. I was responsible for the debts in my name while he was to take care of those in his. I understood this ruling, but it still angered me since he incurred those charges in my name. He was supposed to pay me for court and attorney fees as well as for the back taxes that I paid that were due to his deceptions. I was to be reimbursed for the added cost of carrying him on my health insurance for the previous eight months. The one surprise was the house. I had been trying, through the telephone game of communicating through multiple attorneys, to talk Timothy into selling the house. He had never responded to these inquiries. In court, he made the surprising announcement that he wanted the house which had been sitting vacant and unpaid for the previous eight months. Much of the negotiations were with the mortgage company as a plan was devised. The house would be in his name and he was to refinance to remove my name from the mortgage.

By the time all of the negotiations were complete, it was 4:58, two minutes before the clerk's office closed. As a motley group, we walked the decree to the office to have it stamped and verified prior to the close of business hours. One of my attorneys turned to his.

"So, I can expect a check from your client by the end of the month for his first installment?"

"Only after I get paid," his lawyer responded.

I smiled. This man was finally getting a small taste of what I had been living with. I wanted to tell him with a sweet smile, "Don't worry. I'm sure the check is in the mail."

Walking out of the courthouse, I felt vindicated that the judge seemed to "read him." I was happy that the outcome was in line with what I had hoped. I was angry that, no matter what he was ordered to do and how much "fault" was indicated on the decree, it still was not fair. But, most of all, I was relieved. Relieved that it was over. Relieved that I had reached the summit and bore only minor wounds from the jagged rocks at the peak. Relieved that I could move forward into the vista I assumed would be clearly spread before me.

I knew I still had challenges ahead. After all, I have never been very good at going downhill. But that night was for celebrating, not for worrying about the descent on the other side of the mountain. A group of friends met me at the restaurant that my husband and I had visited on a weekly basis; I was christening it as my own that night. We talked. We laughed. We talked about everything else other than him. The newly minted divorce decree sat in my purse by my feet; I needed to keep the reminder of the reality close at hand.

Not surprisingly, the months following the divorce were not as smooth as I expected. The descent into the rest of my life held some nasty surprises. At this point, I still had faith in the legal system. I had a binding document and no reason to believe that it would not be fulfilled.

He was supposed to pay me several thousand dollars to cover a portion of my attorney fees and to refund the tax debt that I had paid. I received less than $300, one installment. I can't say that I was surprised; after all, that was his M.O. What did surprise me; however, was the response from the courts. Essentially, my only option to try to enforce the decree was to take him back to court, file a civil suit, and get another piece of paper that says he needs to pay. All the while incurring more fees that I would have to pay. No, thank you.

The bigger disappointment came with the house. He never refinanced, never removed my name. I was left in limbo. I was financially liable for a house which I had no rights to. Again, the courts were not supportive.

Following soon after, I received two more tax bills for prior years. Apparently, not only was he not planning on reimbursing me for the first one, he was neglecting these as well (even though the decree made his responsibility here clear). I paid them. At this point, over half my $50,000 salary for the year had gone to attorneys, courts, and the IRS (it would have been nice to earn the $68,000 salary that Timothy claimed for me in his discovery documents).

I had yet another blow as that spring came to a close. I submitted a rental application in preparation to move out of my sanctuary for the recently separated. The application was initially declined due to Timothy not paying the utility bills on the house that was now in his name. Yet another responsibility spelled out in ink on the documents I still carried in my purse. Yet again, I paid.

The unfairness of it all was wearing thin. I felt like he was the teenager who held a big party while the parents were away and I was the guardian left to clean up the mess. The anger was always close to the surface, threatening a tsunami of its own. I felt stuck, trapped by his actions. I raged; how could he continue to hurt me even when we had no legal ties?

I expected that spring to be time to move forward. Instead, that spring was a season for letting go.

I began by letting go of the obvious. Mrs. officially became

Ms., the removal of a single letter that indicated the removal of a partner. I dropped my married name, once again taking on my maiden designation. With this shift, I also cut out much-loved ties to my past, as my former students would now have a more difficult time locating me.

That was just the beginning. Since the day after he left, I had been tracking him online using first the joint account and then his wife's blog. Itemized accounts of his purchases had been replaced by pictures of him with his wife. While he was staying in Atlanta for much of that fall and winter, I would drive by his parent's house every week or so to verify that his car was still in the driveway. Knowing his location made me feel safer; at least I had some information. I also felt like I needed to catalog his actions in case they played a part in the legal process. The day after the legal divorce was the last time I checked her blog, the last time I Googled his name, the last time I tried to find him at all. Even though I had no contact with him for those eight months, he was still in my life as a virtual element. I made the very deliberate choice to never look for him again. His story was no longer connected to mine in any way; I had no reason to continue to follow his actions. I let him go.

I had been relying on medications to help me sleep, eat, and to generally keep the demons sedated. My intention from the beginning was to begin to wean myself off the medication as soon as the divorce was final. I stayed true to plan. With the help of my psychiatrist, I eliminated the Risperdal immediately and began reducing the Celexa. As the drugs left my system, I felt fine. But, I wasn't done. I had left the Trazedone, the sleep-maker, until the end. This was the one whose loss I feared. With the medication, the demons of the night were kept at bay. Once I swallowed those three pills, I knew that I would be in oblivion within the hour. I knew that I could sleep undisturbed by the ghosts of marriage past. I never had to worry about waking to a nightmare about him. I never had to feel the empty side of the bed. I never had to learn to control my anxiety.

The Trazedone was a life preserver for me in the early months. It provided the support I needed at a time when I couldn't do it alone. It was time for me to learn to swim on my own. I began to cut back the dosage. From 300 mg, I dropped to 250 mg for a few days. Then, I reduced it to 200 mg. I continued this pattern until I reached 50 mg. Up to that point, I hadn't noticed too much of a difference. I still fell asleep easily, although I could push through it easier at that point. I woke up occasionally throughout the night, but it was easily manageable. I stayed at that low dose for almost a month, afraid to let go of the life preserver completely. Finally, I released my hold, letting go of the psychological dependence on the medication. I learned to tread water through the dark oceans of the night.

Although I was making progress conquering the night, I still struggled with the succubus of anger throughout the days. I was outraged that he skated through the felony bigamy charge and waltzed unscathed through the civil courts as he continued to ignore the decree with no apparent consequence. Based upon phone calls I received, it seemed as though he had disappeared again; apparently he had grown comfortable with the art of fleeing the scene. I wanted him to pay for his actions. I wanted him to face the consequences of his choices. I didn't need to benefit, but I needed to know. Of course, in order to know, I would either have to hire a private investigator or a psychic, and I was willing to do neither. I had to let go of retribution, give up on consequences, and find peace within the unknown. Slaying the anger would prove to be as difficult as ending Rasputin's life; it refused to die as I refused to give up.

That spring, I also said goodbye to the only school where I had ever worked. I moved out of my friend's home which had been my refuge for the previous year. I set up a new residence thirty miles away, letting go of the community that cradled my married days.

The hardest goodbye of all was nothing tangible, nothing anyone else could even see. Over the previous year, my identity was my divorce, what happened to me. I was the lady whose husband committed bigamy. My stories and updates on the increasingly absurd situation provided entertainment and fodder for those around me. I became the days of their lives. It was a natural role to fill. After all, I needed to talk about what had happened and I happened to have a story that people wanted to hear. In the telling, I gained a thicker skin as the rawness developed into callouses from repetition. I also received comfort, as most listeners were sympathetic, and I was all too eager to paint him as the villain and me as a recipient of his crimes.

I could have kept that identity. Stayed the bigamist's first wife. Remained the victim. There was safety in that role. Security. I knew what it felt like, what the rules were and where the limitations were found. If I chose to shed that identity, it meant that I was responsible for my own happiness. I had to choose my own path and know that, regardless of how it turned out, it was my choice.

For a year, I was the victim trudging up my Kilimanjaro with my burden exposed to the world. I wore my trauma, wanted others to know I was suffering. Now, at the peak, I had a choice. I could continue to trek slowly through the downhill landscape with the heavy pack on my back, or I could choose to release it and trust that I could make it down the mountain alone.

Like I said, I've never been very good at going downhill. But, it was time to learn.

I threw off the pack and trusted gravity to take care of the rest.

Lesson Twelve

Just because a journey is not of one's choosing, it does not mean that it does not have value.

Like many young adults, I looked forward to college. I was tired of the school counselors and the state curriculum telling me what I should learn. I was ready to choose my own classes and my own lessons. When it came time to select my fall courses using the stunted mid-90s technology of phone registration, I punched in course codes that played it safe: physics, architecture, advanced composition, and psychology. All of which played into my interests and proven abilities. I was not challenged. In fact, I took all of the exams for the psychology class in the first week without ever attending a lecture or even buying a book. The 4.0 on my transcript reflected knowledge from a prior time.

I chose my lessons, but I didn't choose the lessons I really needed. Instead, I was drawn to the siren song of practicing the perfect. It is so much more comfortable to walk into a lesson already knowing the answers. To not have to question yourself. To not have to show your ignorance and vulnerabilities. When we are already experts, a lesson becomes food for the ego at the expense of growth for the soul.

Sometimes, the lessons we need the most are the ones we are most resistant to.

Spring 2010

I never wanted to be divorced. That was a fork in the road I never anticipated and never wanted to explore. It was a journey chosen for me and it was a path from which I had much to learn.

A known lesson feeds self-importance. Being unexpectedly thrust into an unfamiliar classroom fuels humility. I thought I knew how to be married. I now had to face the fact that I may not have done that too well and I certainly knew I didn't know how to be single. I felt like I had been catapulted from a graduate course straight back to kindergarten. I needed to start from the beginning learning about myself, my marriage, and relationships in general.

My first lesson was a harsh one. Looking back, I became aware of how much I lived my life on autopilot. I made plans, set them in motion, and then let my mind drift to the next plan, trusting inertia to carry out the current objective. I was an expert navigator with my head bent over the charts and maps, but I rarely occupied the pilot's chair, looking out over the current vistas and enjoying the ride. I planned life rather than living life.

"Just stay in bed with me for a little while," was a common refrain from Timothy on weekend mornings.

He had mastered the art of sleeping in; this plea was usually uttered after 10:00 as I went back in the bedroom to rouse him. By 10:00, I had been up for four or five hours and usually had half my list for the day knocked out and was anxious to begin the next half.

"I'll try," I would often reply, snuggling in next to him as I picked up my book de jour, determined not to waste a moment's time.

On the best of these mornings, he would curl up next to me, his leg over mine. His hand would begin to wander and the marital bed would be put to good use. Even then, in the post-coital glow, I could not simply *be*. Once my senses returned and I was confident that my legs would support me, I would get up, get showered, and move on with the day. My autopilot engaged once again.

I was so busy planning at times that I forgot to live. So caught up in thinking that I forgot to feel. I was so focused on "down the road" that I not only didn't smell the roses, I wasn't even aware of their existence.

My lack of mindfulness was also a way to avoid pain. I first realized how dependent I had become upon my ability to disassociate, and to let my mind travel away from whatever discomfort I was currently experiencing when I would not let myself truly feel the sadness born from the end of my marriage. I kept my mind reigned in, under tight control. I had a top-shelf mental spam filter. If I sensed that it was tiptoeing too closely to emotions that I did not want to feel, I immediately distracted it with action or conscious thought.

This approach served me well for a while after the divorce; it allowed me to survive without being flattened by the despair brought on by the sudden loss. As with anything we repeatedly do, mental disconnection can become a habit. I became adept at avoiding the sadness. However, as long as I avoided the pain, I prevented the healing.

Mindfulness is a highlighter. It shows us what is causing discomfort; it reveals patterns of connection and disconnection.

Mindfulness is a clue that something about that environment, situation, or relationship may need to change because it is causing you pain. Or, perhaps, you need to be honest with yourself about the discomfort and change your approach to it. Regardless, mentally running away from any lasting situation will not be of benefit. Bring your focus to the present and connect with what is causing you discomfort. As with studying a textbook, the highlighted areas are the ones that need more attention.

One area in my life was wet with fluorescent ink: my sight.

1985

I knew that I couldn't see very well. I had to squint to read the board and I sat too close to the T.V. I did not realize how poor my vision was until I had my first optometrist appointment in third grade. He performed the usual tests asking me to read lines of print and look into bright lights. He mumbled and made notations on my chart. He looked surprised at some of the readings, but never articulated why. A few days later, my dad took me back to pick up my new glasses. I slid the purple plastic frames onto my face and looked out the expanse of windows at the parking lot beyond.

"There are leaves on the trees!" I called out in excitement to the entire store. All of the adults laughed and exchanged knowing smiles. They had experience with seeing and not-seeing, whereas I only knew what it was like to be blind.

Spring 2010

When my husband left, I put on my glasses. I saw him with more clarity and I could see myself without the fuzzy edges of myopia. Sometimes the view was harsh but that was the reality. I looked at my marriage with vision corrected by perspective. I examined how I really felt within the marriage and with the man I loved.

"You make me happy."

I used to say those words to my husband on a frequent basis. At that time, if you had asked me what I meant by those four words, I would have replied that I was saying that I loved him and that I was happy being with him. I meant those words as a compliment, an endearment, an expression of love.

I don't use those words anymore.

If he made me happy, then how could I be happy without him?

I began to realize that by telling him that he made me happy, I was putting all of the responsibility for my own well-being on his shoulders. That is a huge burden to carry and one that was unfair to him. I had given him the power to make me happy. Which means he also had the power to make me unhappy.

If I had left that power in his hands, he would have packed up my happiness with the rest of his belongings when he walked out the door. I snatched it back from him, determined to find a way to regain ownership of my well-being.

I now take responsibility for my own happiness. I can choose how I respond and how I approach. I can choose to be happy with or happy in spite of. That is my responsibility. But, coffee still *makes* me happy!

Summer 2008

Soon after moving into our home in 2000, I began to dream of turning our almost-acre of untamed weeds and sporadic trees into a woodland garden. We began by planting a single tree, a bald cypress that reminded us of the Texas Hill Country where we had spent the summers of our youth. This was a nursery-grown plant in a five-gallon bucket. We were determined to give it the best start possible. We began to dig a hole, intending a pit a couple of feet deep and five feet or so in diameter. We were surprised by sparks just a few inches below the soil, and our original hole gained dimension as we had to remove a leftover sewer ring that had found its way into our yard. We carefully mixed the Georgia native red clay with manure to create a better growing medium. We then placed the three-foot tree in the middle of the now 10-foot diameter hole and back-filled the soil until the tree was firmly anchored in place. Next, we encircled the tree with a wire fence to keep the dogs and the deer away from the delicate branches.

I took great care of that initial tree. I carefully teased out weeds that ventured too close, trimmed the branches to ensure a strong foundation, and supplemented water in the hot Georgia summers. Soon, I realized that a single young tree, no matter how well tended, would not go far to create my woodland dream.

The next spring, I ordered dozens of one-foot saplings from

the forestry service and I supplemented them with hydrangea cuttings from the neighbor. By this time, the plants had overwhelmed our ability to provide vigilant care. We took on a new attitude towards planting: dig a small hole with loosed dirt around the pit, sprinkle manure on top and let the worms do the work of mixing it in, and let the strongest survive. Although our new, more cavalier, attitudes did cause some plants to die (or disappear overnight in the case of deer raids), our garden began to grow.

Over the next few years, I spent my spare moments painting with plants: the strong lines of tree trunks contrasting with the soft spray of the delicate astilbe flowers, the strong punch of hosta interspersed with lacey fronds and self-spreading blooms. Slowly, the young trees grew to create an understory and the ground-hugging plants won the battle against the weeds. I loved my garden. I would sit in the hammock and watch the rabbits weave in and out of the shrubs, avoiding the dogs' detection. The butterflies covered the lantana and the birds made nests in the vines. The entire yard was dappled shade, as the maturing trees blocked out the harsh southern sun. I had my woodland dream.

A piece of that dream disintegrated in the summer of 2008, when a strong storm blew down one of the mature sweetgum trees that sheltered a large swath of sensitive shade-loving plants. As I cleaned up the debris and moved the huge slabs of trunk out of the way, tears welled up at the loss of my favorite area of the garden. I felt my heart curl as the delicate leaves rolled up in defense of the jarring rays now beating down upon them. I felt as though my years of effort were wasted, undone with a single crack of a tree.

The next morning found me yet again surveying the wreckage,

the damaged plants barely hanging on to life. With a burst of energy, I decided to take action. I carefully dug up each exposed plant and moved it to a new home in a suitable locale that would still offer the needed shade. One by one, I relocated almost a hundred shrubs and flowers until all that remained was a large area of bare earth.

I had salvaged what I could, but now it was time to truly embrace what I had seen as a disaster. After washing off the soil clinging to my limbs, I curled up on my favorite chair with a stack of gardening books. I looked through pages of sun-loving plants, thrilled at the variety and color that my newly exposed yard could now support. Within a few weeks, the signs of the destruction were muted and the debris field had been filled with riotous color and exuberant growth.

I took that early lesson in my garden and tried to apply it to my own life years later. I may not have asked to be exposed to harsh realities of life, but I surely wasn't going to curl up and die when I could learn to create joy out of the devastation. I wanted to end my own dark ages with my own enlightenment.

Lesson Thirteen

Layering isn't just for sweaters.

Several years ago, Timothy and I were on the interstate heading out on our weekly Costco run. The roads were packed and traffic was doing that infuriating start-stop thing where we averaged about 0.87 mph. I took that opportunity to share the information from an article I had read that applied the theory of fluid dynamics to traffic congestion. I was excited about the research, animated. I used the cars around us to demonstrate the ideas in the research about how traffic jams started, why they perpetuated, and how they could be resolved. Since his science passions tended towards the astronomical and his mathematical knowledge was limited to the calculations needed for computer graphics, he did not share my enthusiasm for the article. In fact, he thought it was nonsense. From that point forward, every time we were stuck in traffic, he would make a joke about "damn fluid dynamics." It became part of our shared past.

Timothy and I were both only children. We moved across the country at a young age and lost touch with our childhood friends. Due to geographical constraints and age differences, neither one of us was close to our respective cousins. Our relationship was the only one we had that spanned the decades of our lives. As a result, many of our memories existed in a vault where we possessed the only keys.

We filled that repository with thousands of shared experiences,

289

stories, and jokes. We grew to where we could communicate complex commentary with a few short words or a wriggle of the brow. Situations would trigger the same recollections in each of us, and we often found ourselves pronouncing some thought in unison. We would generously pull from our vault of memories, retelling stories from our history.

The end of the marriage was the death of our shared past.

I was struck with the reality when, only three days after the text that ensured our days of creating memories together were over, I overheard a remark that played in to one of our long standing jokes. Without any conscious thought, I typed out a text to him relaying the comment. I stopped before I hit "send," realizing the magnitude of the loss for first time. The vault, which we had filled for 16 years and visited regularly, was now filled with relics of the past quickly collecting dust.

For months, I avoided the catacombs that contained the memories and dreams of a fallen marriage. I drove circuitous routes to avoid our old neighbourhood, I went out of my way to visit unfamiliar stores, and I stubbornly attempted to block any uninvited recollections by carefully controlling any internal or external stimulus. I tried living within self-imposed boundaries, designed to safeguard me from thoughts of him and our shared past.

I wanted to be able to tour the museum of our marriage, gaze upon its creations, even if it was to be a lonely tour. There was beautiful artwork there, although now I questioned its authenticity. Was its beauty any less if it was a fraud? Was it only valuable if it was genuine? Or did it only matter that it was real to me, the joy in the perception rather than in the intention of the creator?

As I wrestled with these questions, I worked to layer new memories atop the old, not to bury the former, but to soften it with the extra coating helping to shield me from the cold. I drug new city-dwelling friends on hikes through familiar mountain trails, each footstep marring Timothy's a little more. I took dates to "our" restaurant, intentionally guiding them to sit where he once did. Their weight helped to press him out. I had a standing Tuesday night appointment with Christian when we would watch *Lost*, first catching up on the old seasons in preparation for the new. I watched Sawyer's character closely, looking for signs of my husband in the practiced con man. These were all familiar patterns with unfamiliar people.

I took a lesson from Cesar Milan, the Dog Whisperer, seeing myself in the fearful dogs afraid to confront the object that causes them distress. Cesar would not force the dog to interact with the dreaded object, rather he would encourage the dog to relax, to take on a calm submissive state around the anxiety trigger. I applied that same lesson to myself. I grew ever more comfortable with the memories; I learned to relax around them rather than tense up in fear or avoid them altogether.

It was a surreal time. The ghost of Timothy accompanied me on every outing, and joined me in every conversation. He was always there, yet said nothing. No task, no matter how small, escaped his presence. He hid at the grocery store, taunting me behind his favorite brand of sparkling water. He joined me for dinner when my companion ordered his favorite beer. He sat along side me as I watched the final season of *Lost*, only this time he did not engage in discourse about the storyline. He was in my past, yet he refused to stay there.

Summer 2010

A year passed. Anniversaries knocked against my still-fragile mind like branches against an unsheltered window in a storm. Three hundred and sixty-six days after I lost my husband, I again stood in front of the security line at Atlanta's Hartsfield-Jackson airport. One year ago, I stood ensconced in my husband's arms for the last time before I left to reconnect with my father. One year hence, I stood with my new boyfriend, trying not to crumple under the memories as he embraced me before sending me on my way to see my mother's side of the family. My past, present, and future all collided in front of the TSA poster that advised travelers about carry-on restrictions. I wasn't worried about the contents of my bag; I was still carrying dangerous cargo in my heart.

It became difficult to separate harmless memories, residue of past attacks from legitimate concerns in the present moment. Expectations were set, not based upon fact, but upon tenacious whispers from my history. It was a dangerous precedent; if I expected the past to repeat itself, I would be providing fertile ground for more betrayal to grow. This was highlighted for me upon my return from that summer trip; I realized when I saw my boyfriend's car pull up at the curb outside baggage claim that I was partially expecting him not to show. He had never proven himself untrustworthy. But then again, neither had my husband.

Relieved, I reached up to give him a hug, "It's great to see you."

Hugging me back, "I missed you," he replied.

Once inside the car, I admitted, "I halfway expected you not to show."

He looked shocked, hurt. "Why would you think that?" he said, a hard edge sliding into his voice. "I told you I'd come get you."

"I know," I replied softly, feeling ashamed. "It's just that last year..." I trailed off.

"I'm not him."

Of course, I knew that on a rational level; I never consciously compared them. It was a matter of memories coursing through my bloodstream, igniting stress hormones that, in turn, sent false signals of impending doom. I also knew that this was dangerous territory; if I expected others to behave like Timothy, eventually they would.

I wondered when I would be healed, all wounds sealed over with pink new skin stretched taut over the torment. I repeatedly reached a point where I thought I was cured, only to have the fragile derma torn open again as it caught on a reminder of the betrayal and loss. I have since reached the conclusion that, at least for me, "healed" is unattainable. I am healing always. It gets easier every day and the rough patches are smoother and shorter than before, but I don't think they will ever be gone completely. All I can hope for is that I will continue to improve at navigating the difficult times while always being thankful for the much more numerous wonderful times.

I am aided in my healing by that great river of time. She is slowly swallowing up or eroding away many of the tangible reminders of a shared past. The phone, which announced the terminal point of my marriage, was replaced with a new one courtesy of my boyfriend. My hands were no longer subjected to the familiar form of the old phone and my mind was not exposed to the visual reminder of the fateful text. My computer, a hand-me-down from Timothy that still bore his name on every application and registration, was replaced with a newer model. I received news that my Max, the impish pug that signalled the start of my marriage, had been put to sleep after her medical conditions began to cause her too much distress. The clothes that wrapped my body through my marriage wore out piece by piece and were replaced with garments that never hung along side his. My car, the 1999 Integra we bought as soon as I moved to Atlanta, will not run forever and I will no longer listen to the radio that his hands patiently installed for me. My cat, the only animal I kept from my old life, is nearing the end of hers. One by one, the old threads are being snipped away, leaving room for new layers to be woven on top.

But, still I mourn the death of our shared past. The memories that peek out beneath the sweaters.

Lesson Fourteen

Choose to be a student of life rather than a victim of circumstance.

1993

I was born with some unusual anatomy in my wrists; the transverse carpal ligaments placed excessive pressure on my median nerves long before I had accumulated the necessary hours for a repetitive stress injury. After many frustrating appointments over many long years, a nerve conduction test was finally ordered. The results were clear; the ligament on my dominant right hand would need to be cut.

Surgery was scheduled for the winter of my fourteenth year. The procedure itself was straightforward, but the recovery was more difficult than anticipated. I spent months in rehab trying to regain any strength and sensation in the misbehaving hand. Finally, tired of spending my days with elderly stroke victims playing therapy basketball with wrist weights hanging off my arms, I looked for new options.

On a whim, I looked up fencing in the San Antonio phone book, inspired by the swordplay antics of the Monkees and *The Princess Bride's* "Sweet" Wesley's skill with a blade. Alongside countless ads for chain links and white pickets, I found what I was looking for: Salle Pouj. Gerard "Pouj" Poujardieu, Jr. was a gruff Frenchman who had ____ been coaching champion fencers for years.

I was immediately captivated by the thought of swords and boys in tight pants.

"Mom, I think I found what I want to do to help my hand heal," knowing that approaching the request from a healing perspective rather than from a desire to wield a weapon would help my case.

"What's that?" she asked, with no clue as to what was to come.

"Fencing," I replied with a grin.

"You mean, with swords? Real swords? Oh, Lisa," her face at once grimacing and falling.

"Can we at least check it out?"

The next week, my mom and I entered the salle for the first time, my enthusiasm in counterpoint to her trepidation.

Pouj addressed her first, taking her hand lightly in his and bringing to his lips for a quick kiss, "It is lovely to meet you, young lady."

This guy was good. My 44 year old divorced mother blushed and mumbled something unintelligible in return.

My mom was no match for Pouj's flirtations and my pleas; I started fencing lessons within the month. My weapon of choice was the foil which, at just over a pound, was a challenge for my healing wrist and hand.

Much to Pouj's delight, it turned out I had a knack for fencing. I quickly adapted to the footwork and pacing and learned to use my short stature to my advantage. The medals began to mount as I honed my skills on the strip. The frailty and pain in my hand continued to be my one shortcoming; I was scared to push too hard and faced hours of discomfort when I did push.

Pouj finally tired of my complaints. "Do you want to cry, or do you want to win?"

I wanted to win.

Summer 2010

My divorce was a tsunami, a great wave arising from a previously placid sea that destroys all in its path. The precursors to the giant wave were hidden deep beneath the surface of the marital waters and were not visible to the naked eye. As I did not possess the equipment needed to warn of its approach, I was caught unawares while standing on that beautiful beach. The shock wave of the sudden departure of my husband carried me far inland, depositing me in a foreign world, unrecognizable.

I was flattened. Nearly drowned. I cursed the battering ram of water that sought to destroy me and all I knew. I raged at the unfairness. I spent time curled on the wave-swept beach afraid to stand up again.

"Look what this evil force did to me!" I wanted to scream, my voice carrying out over land and sea.

"See this? This powerful wave hid its nature, encouraged complacency on the sunny shore, and then it burst forth, tearing up roots and carrying me to unknown locals in its watery belly. And, then? Then, it folded back into the sea as though it had never been there at all."

"Look at me! I am left here alone on the shore that once housed my marriage. I thought it was a beautiful marriage. I had no chance to save it, no way to fight or even run from the violent surf."

It was all too easy to see myself as a casualty of the

destructive force, a sacrifice made and washed away. I could have easily stood amongst the debris, blaming him for the state of my life.

Rather than curse the wave, I looked to the purification of the flood. Instead of focusing on the debris, I looked to the possibilities.

Fall 2010

My plans to escape the toxic memories held in Atlanta had been modified. One of the men on the spreadsheet had managed to become much more than simply data in a spreadsheet cell. I saw promise, potential, and possibilities for a new life in an old city. As a teacher, I was bound by the school calendar, locked into a location like a pin on a map from August to May each year. I elected to take a chance: to find a job and a home in the city I had vowed to leave. My need to flee had been tempered by time, and my interest in new romance had been piqued.

I moved into my own apartment, the first time I had ever truly lived alone. As I had sold my old furniture as part of my old life I needed to leave behind, I delighted in choosing pieces from IKEA to populate my new space. I selected furniture scaled to my petite frame, no longer concerned with accommodating Timothy's 6'1" stature. I found myself drawn to designs that were in utter contrast to the style I embraced in my former life: dark woods and strong lines replaced with white painted tables and bright accents.

Strangely, I found myself most excited about the kitchen, a small Formica-filled space that stood in sharp contrast to the custom, stone-filled space Timothy and I had build together in our old home. My former kitchen, although functional and beautiful, was underutilized. I never saw cooking or food preparation as important. I had been an almost lifelong vegetarian and Timothy was practically a carnivore. I preferred to eat dinner early, whereas he frequently consumed his main meal after 8:00 p.m. As a result of our divergent diets and busy, yet child-free schedules, we survived on frozen meals and easy-to-prepare foods.

My attitude towards food began to shift during the year I lived with Sarah. I started to see value in food beyond the counts of macronutrients and a palatable flavor. I began to see the value in nourishing myself with real food rather then simply consuming my daily rations. I saw the time in the kitchen as an investment in myself and in my health. I became interested in the social aspect of sustenance, and I yearned to be able to cook for others.

The first night in my new apartment found me making gluten-free brownies from scratch while in my underwear as I celebrated the space and freedom accorded by my own space. That little generic kitchen supported me as I tried new recipes and experimented with my own. I went from being an ignorant chef to being the go-to person for all things vegetarian and gluten-free and, in the process, I learned the importance of nourishing the body.

I designed my apartment to be a space that fostered mental healing as well. Soft blankets and warm candlelight belied the turmoil that still roiled in my head.

As I was settling in to my new, more independent life, I was still struggling to figure out where the divorce belonged in my life. I had long ago accepted that I was no longer the Mrs., and probably not even missed, but I was still having trouble seeing myself apart from my role as the bigamist's first wife.

I began to see my life as a story, a play in multiple acts. The story opened with my childhood, a relatively normal and uneventful chapter punctuated by my willful actions. My childhood was followed with a brief, but tumultuous act that was characterized by loss: my parent's divorce, my dad's move across the country, and the unexpected deaths of many friends. The third act encompassed my entire adult life thus far: from sixteen to thirty-two. Initially, I viewed both of us as characters in some twisted romance turned psychological drama. He, of course, was the antagonist, performing all sorts of unspeakable acts towards me while I remained clueless. I was fearful of turning each page, afraid of what horrors would await me. I felt powerless, victimized.

Then I realized, although I may not possess the power to write my entire story, I can shift into the position of the narrator. I have the ability to interpret his actions, guide the story, and shift the focus on the past. I could not control the actions of the antagonist, but I could surely control how I wove them into the story. This guise also allows me to step back from the action, gaining perspective and a broader view.

I became the director, limiting Timothy's time on the stage of my life. I could not change his actions during the third act, but I would not allow that to be the end of the tale, nor would I allow him to have a major role in the acts yet to come. He had his mark, and he certainly helped to shape the story, but he does not need to occupy space on the stage; he is now relegated to the shadows of the wings.

The curtains closed briefly between acts. I spent time lost in the darkness behind their folds, unsure how to proceed. One of the hardest parts about being betrayed is that you feel like a fool, a failure. You question yourself endlessly. I blamed me almost as much as I blamed him. My self-image was in question; I had never perceived myself as naïve, as a patsy. I was intelligent and independent. Observant. Or, at least that was how I saw myself before.

I wanted to punish myself, berate myself endlessly for my stupidity and my gullibility. I alternated between wanting to self-flagellate for not recognizing his pain and wanting to lash out at the indignity of being deceived. I needed to issue myself a pardon, exonerate myself for my part. And, somehow, I knew I needed to forgive him as well.

Forgiveness is such a loaded word.

It requires an acceptance of someone's actions. Actions that may be horrific, born from unknown motivations. How could I excuse years of lies? Was I supposed to ignore the wedding vows that pledged his love to another written while he still claimed to love me? Should I disregard his attacks through the Last Con letter and his attorney as he painted me as a greedy, vindictive shrew?

It was an unfathomable thing to do. I viewed forgiveness as a selfless act, and I had a self that was way too hurt to pardon its executioner. I couldn't begin to even understand what he did much less WHY he did. And, now, I was supposed to exonerate him for those same things? It just seemed like one more way that he would be getting away with his choices and actions. I refused to endorse his behavior with my stamp of approval.

Time passed. He remained unforgiven. I thought I could attend to my anger without addressing that little matter of absolution. I was wrong. I held on to an ember of hate, fueled by my refusal to accept his choices. I held onto the image of him scorching in the ninth level of hell, reserved for those accused of treachery in Dante's Inferno.

I grew to see forgiveness in a different light. It was actually a selfish act for me. After all, I do not expect to ever have any contact with him again. He will never know if I am his pardoner or if I hunt for vengeance. I forgave him for me. It helped to extinguish the fire of anger. It brought peace to my days and kept him out of my dreams at night.

In order to find forgiveness, I had to shift my view of him. I had to see him as sick, confused, desperate. I do not know how true any or all of those labels are, but they are true to me as they helped me to feel compassion for him. They let me accept that my greatest love sought to destroy me, regardless of intent. I cling to those labels when I feel the anger spark. I cover the ember with thoughts of mental illness and a frantic push to survive. I chose to see him as weak and frightened, acting in his own twisted version of self defense, rather than as some evil puppet-master cruelly controlling my life. He had some twisted origami of depression, folding inward and outward until it created a grotesque form.

I do not endorse his choices. Regardless of his mental state, he lied and manipulated for years, he committed bigamy and fraud, and he ran and hid like a frightened coward. I still believe that he belongs in prison for his actions. I still would feel no sadness if I heard of his demise. I have simply found a way let go in my mind so that I could find peace.

I have forgiven him, but I will never forget the pain. I've buried the hatchet, but I've marked its location. And I can't promise he'll be safe if he ever faces me in a fencing match.

Lesson Fifteen

There is no limit to the number of times you can reframe something.

April 2000

I lay sleeping in the backseat of the realtor's car, ensconced in a Benadryl coma prompted by the extreme pollen that moves into Atlanta in the spring like an alien invasion.

"Lisa, wake up. We're here," came Timothy's voice from the passenger seat.

With an unbecoming grunt, I lifted myself to a semi-upright position only to see a rotten garage door, overgrown weeds with a sprinkling of grass, and an assortment of broken pots haphazardly scattered around the entrance to the home.

"No way," I exclaimed, still trying to shake off the effects of the antihistamine. "We don't even need to look inside; this place is terrible."

"Let's give it a chance," stated Timothy calmly, extending a hand to help me out of the car.

Upon entering the vacant house, my eye first went to the outdated parquet floor in the entranceway. Feeling validated, I turned to say something to Timothy when my gaze went out the back windows to a glorious, huge wooded and private backyard. The ugly front yard and disappointing foyer forgotten, I ran to the back deck with a huge grin on my face, surveying the beautiful expanse of green.

Our eyes met, both sets sparkled from behind lids crinkled from our huge smiles. This was it. It was home.

The rest of the house, although possessing the required basics, was hideous. It had been a rental for a few years and then vacant for one. It was almost 15 years old and had never had so much as a pedicure, much less a facelift.

None of that mattered. We got a great deal on the house and immediately set about making it our own beginning by ripping up all the floors mere hours after closing, much to the shock of our realtor. Over the 10 years we spent in the house, we redid every room, some more than once. We worked as a great team: he rolled and I painted trim, he mortared and I grouted, he cut and I measured.

Rather than simply accept the house for what it was, we reframed it one wall and floor at a time until it was a space we loved.

Fall 2010

The renovation I faced that fall had nothing to do with home construction. I was facing a major life renovation. My old life had been stripped down to the essential supports needed for survival. For more than a year, these posts and beams were enough. But now that I had crossed the finish line of the divorce, moved into my own place, and started a new job. I was ready to build again.

I had to examine the old structure with a critical eye; I did not want to build on a weak foundation as I unknowingly did with the marriage.

I began to reframe, choosing to focus on what I gained with the receipt of the text rather than allowing the loss to be the cornerstone of my life. That summer, I may have lost a husband, but I gained a father.

My parent's divorce occurred when I was in elementary school. My dad then relocated across the country shortly after I turned 11. We did not see much of each other for the rest of my childhood or throughout my twenties. In fact, we didn't really know each other.

In the summer of 2009, I went to visit my dad in Seattle for the first time in several years. I think we were both a little nervous as were trying to learn the choreography of our adult relationship. We made some tenuous inroads on the first part of the trip. As we kayaked Lake Union, hiked Cougar Mountain, and rode the flight simulator at the Museum of Flight, we were starting to open up to each other.

He was by my side when I received the text that ended my marriage. In that instant, I gained a father in the truest sense of the word.

With no hesitation, I became his little girl again. He moved into action immediately doing what he could. He held my hand for the endless trip back to Atlanta not even letting go when he drifted off to sleep on the plane. He made the phone calls I couldn't and stayed in the house with the dogs when I wasn't able. He cried with me and cursed with me. He hurt with me and he healed with me.

I may have lost a husband, but I gained a father. A guide. A cheerleader. A mentor. A friend.

I began to see my divorce as a gift. A gift I never asked for, and one I never wanted, but since it came with a "no return policy," I was determined to make the best of it. The scarlet letter emblazoned across my forehead that inspired shame when I admitted to a failed marriage was repurposed as a red badge of courage, a mark that showed that I had loved and lived to love again.

I received validation from the strangest of places beginning with the Internal Revenue Service. Timothy had always been the one to manage the taxes for us; although I was a math teacher, I never possessed the patience to navigate through form 1040 and line item A. As with our other finances, I trusted him after so many years together and I relied upon his verbal synopsis of the outcome each spring. Apparently, Timothy had begun to see the federal reserve as his own private bank as he manipulated the documents to garner large, and undeserved returns. Returns that were direct deposited and quickly scurried away before I ever even knew of their existence.

Within a few days of The Great Disappearance of 2009, I received the first of many notices from the IRS. It was quickly apparent that he had not been disputing a false charge, but in fact had been running from the results of a valid audit. He had tried to conceal the audit through the removal of all of the tax-related documentation from the home. Soon after he left, I requested past tax returns for the previous several years. I was seething. How dare he leave me with this while he was off gallivanting around? I wrote my first of many checks to the IRS that day, using the first of the sampler checks that came with my new checking account. Over the next two years, I was to send them thousands, each check ripping a hole, letting my anger bubble to the surface again.

My dad came to the rescue with an e-mail sent after one particularly painful check.

"Have you heard of this? It may be helpful." Below, there was a link to the IRS's Innocent Spouse Program.

The program had been designed to offer tax relief to spouses who were victims of abuse or fraud. I was hopeful, but the statistics were not on my side; only a small number of applicants were approved. Undaunted, I began the ugly task of compiling evidence and telling my story. The huge plastic bucket that contained all of the paperwork associated with the July tsunami and its subsequent day in court stood prominently in my apartment living room. I sorted its contents again, touching many of the pages for the first time in a year. I built my case again, hoping for better results this time around.

Finally, after days of copying documents, filling out forms, and writing my story, I mailed off a thick package that I hoped would return at least some of the money to me. I had no idea at the time that the money wasn't the important part.

Months later, I received a notice that I had a certified letter ready for pick-up. My stomach dropped, as I had been conditioned to certified letters signaling more money owed or another bomb ready to drop. When the postmistress placed the stocky envelope in my hands, she uttered an apology.

"Sorry. It's from the IRS. Nobody likes to get those."

I thanked her and moved to the side of the room bracing myself against the green tiled wall as I slid my finger under to the flap to break the seal.

"We have determined that you are eligible for Innocent Spouse Relief."

I let out a sharp cry as I slid to the floor, grasping the stapled pages in both hands. The tears began, falling from my eyes that tracked that single line again and again. The postmistress looked up, concerned. Leaving her current customer, she lifted the hinged counter section, kneeled next me, and inquired about my well-being.

"I'm great," I said through the sobs. "I got Innocent Spouse Relief. The IRS gave me the justice the courts never did."

"That's great, honey," she replied, looking equal parts relieved and confused.

Hours went by before I was able to read more than that single sentence. There was a 90-day waiting period where Timothy would have a chance to contest before they would issue a check. I did not care. I was fixated on that single word, "Innocent." After enduring the months of attacks by Timothy and his attorney, and internalizing some his lies, I felt such relief at the conclusion reached by a third party.

I had long since given up my faith in labels, but that simple declaration from the IRS freed me from bonds I was not aware ensnared me, releasing me in the way that I expected from the court ruling.

I became conscious of the fact that I was more malleable than I ever realized. I was not destroyed by the tsunami that swept over me, but I was changed completely and inexorably. While attending a wellness conference after the divorce, I once again took the Myers-Briggs personality inventory. The results objectified what I had suspected; I was no longer the same person. I had shifted from a "thinking" place to more of a "feeling" one. I still was a big picture builder, but now I looked to human values and motivations as well as data and technology. It was there in black and white; I was more balanced than before.

Sometimes, you have to have the world stripped down to the studs in order to realize that you are unbalanced. Luckily, there is no limit to the number of times you can reframe something.

Lessons From the End of a Marriage

Lesson Sixteen

Soften to those things which cause you discomfort.

When I was a toddler, I used to try to walk through the sliding glass door. Repeatedly. The coffee table was simply an apparition that should bend to my will and allow me passage. Even the bulk of the couch was no match for my determination; I assumed that it too could be bested if I tried long enough and hard enough.

As I approached adulthood and learned about the states of matter, I realized that my chances of walking through solids were pretty slim. However, this did little to temper my tenacity and stubbornness. These traits saw me through many challenges in my life; I succeeded because I refused to give up. I worked to make myself stronger, both physically and emotionally to see me through the challenges that life had to offer. I had perseverance and reliance in droves.

It wasn't enough. At least not for the long run.

1994

My first lesson in softness came from Timothy as he taught me the value in being touched. Even as a young child, I resisted physical affection. I would pull away as even the slighted contact was overwhelming to me, sending my sensitive nerve endings into turmoil.

311

I became an expert in half-hugs and rolling out from under unwanted embraces. As I entered my teen years, I found I enjoyed touch of a sexual nature, but that I would still shut down if affection was communicated through contact.

Timothy sought to change that. He started slowly, sitting behind me in the kitchen chair, lightly embracing me as I engulfed my after school meal and rarely being near me without a hand or foot grazing my body. I grew comfortable. I learned to relax into his arms, to enjoy the feeling of my body intertwined with his. When I was anxious, he would pull my body atop his skin to skin with my ear over his heart, and my own respirations would slow as his calm energy flowed through me. I softened to his touch.

Physical affection became a hallmark of our relationship. We always parted ways with an embrace and greeted each other in a similar fashion. We moved in concert, comfortable in the puzzles of our bodies fitting together just so. We used touch to communicate love and lust, comfort and longing, familiarity and excitement. I was still strong. Too strong at times. But I had learned the first touch of softness in his arms.

Fall 2010

My strength got me through the early days and months of my divorce. I looked to my fortitude to help me push through what seemed like insurmountable obstacles. By that fall, more than a year after I had collapsed on the floor, I had come through quite a journey according to all external indications.

Then, one day, I realized the external barriers were gone. I had completed my amateur jobs of private investigator and paralegal. The civil and criminal trials were behind me. I had moved on physically with a new job and a new home. All that was left were my interior barriers, and try as I might, I couldn't simply lower my head and barrel through them. This was not a time for strength.

My earliest lesson in softening came that first fall, mere months after the initial blow. I knew I needed help, and that I needed new tools in my kit. I signed up for a three-day meditation and yoga retreat run by an unknown therapist whose sparkling eyes spoke to me across the internet. I had a feeling this sanctuary in the North Georgia Mountains held some of the answers that I was seeking.

As it turned out, I was first in need of a remedial class: Basic Breath for Dummies. I lay on the carpeted floor in the therapist's room, a soft warm blanket covering my still-rigid body. She sat next to me on the floor, speaking gently, guiding me. She began by drawing my attention to my breath, the great sustainer of life that I ignored while bound in the swaddling cloth of grief. The first intake of air was shallow, my chest barely lifting with each inhale, as I strained against the straight jacket of sorrow. The breath fought for space in my tight chest, my intercostal muscles tensing as though under assault. Encouraged by her words and feeling safe under the caress of the blanket, I tentatively filled my lungs with air, breathing deep into my chest for the first time in months. I was afraid of what would happen if I allowed the air to take hold, to fill the spaces deep within. I exhaled. Tried again, getting a little deeper this time.

I spent almost a half hour on her floor allowing myself to breathe. Allowing the bindings on the stress-induced corset to unravel. Allowing myself to feel. Giving permission to the breath to enter and accepting its presence.

This was a valuable lesson, but one that I soon forgot as I reentered the real world outside the retreat center. I needed more than a short class; I needed lasting wisdom, and when it comes to breathing, I am a slow learner.

2011

I first started lifting weights during my freshman year in high school. I was fighting for control over my body after undergoing hand surgery that left me more dependent than a teenager ever wants to be. As I grew older and bolder, I increased the poundage until I was comfortable swinging 45 pound plates around.

Lifting was a way to force my mind to rest. I could stay within my comfort zone of strength training and yet flirt with meditation behind the scenes. When executing a compound movement with heavy weight, my mind could not wander; the monkey that normally scurried around the folds of my cortex was silenced under the burden. Breath was forced into the smallest bronchi as the body demanded extra oxygen. Each flexion of muscle was accompanied by a relaxation of mind, a perfect partnership of mind and body.

For many years, the weight room was my only practice with mindfulness. Using weights as the sole tool to calm my mind was essentially like trying to encourage a wingless kiwi to undertake a transatlantic flight simply by screaming at the hapless bird. It will try and it might have limited success, but it will not be able to go the long haul. It is much better to simply select a better bird from the outset.

I eventually found the much-needed wisdom on the yoga mat, although it took time for the lessons to hold. As I bent my body into impossible folds, exploring the edge of what my tendons could bear, my mind began to shift as well.

I was taught that yoga is not goal-oriented, that the way one moves into a pose is as important, if not more important, than the pose itself. Competition within the class was discouraged both between yogis and within yourself. I was encouraged to listen to my body each day and accept it where it was in that moment. I learned that when I felt stressed in a pose or when the discomfort mounted, I had a tendency to forget to breathe. I did that off the yoga mat as well.

The instructor taught me to be aware of the tension in my body and to relax the pull in one area without transferring it to another. I thought about my life – how often had I allowed stress in one sector to bleed into another? Although I thought I was doing better at lowering tension, I was actually just growing more adept at stress transference, and not letting it settle in any one place for too long.

In yoga, I learned that when I faced a challenge with my mind, when I gritted my teeth and tried to force through the barrier, I became stuck. Frozen in both body and brain. Up until this point, I had always tried to use my mind to teach my body. I realized that the lessons move both ways.

My lightbulb moment came when we were in a twisted crescent lunge and asked to add a bind, where the arms wrap around the body in such a way that it causes the mind to panic as it attempts to work out the necessary geometry to adopt the pose without dislocating a shoulder. I was deep in my lunge, attempting to grasp my hands under my leg with my arm around my back when I shut down. I locked up tighter than a bank at midnight. The instructor, sensing my distress, came over and grasped my arms. While moving them into position, she whispered, "Breathe." My hands touched and my mind opened. We switched to the other side. This time, I let my body show my brain what to do and I moved into the pose easily.

A physical bind in yoga provides a safe place for the mind to practice untying cognitive knots: twisted thoughts turned in upon themselves. With gentle pressure and a patient hand, these labyrinthine unravel into a sense of clarity.

Through yoga I am learning to accept suffering and not be fearful of my edge. I am learning to recognize pain as a temporary state. I am discovering that when I breathe into the unease, soften into its arms, I reduce the discomfort. I practice this weekly as I have a tendency to easily forget this lesson.

Even with the yoga, my monkey mind still held court in my brain. He was a merciless ruler, throwing thoughts and screeching in fear. My monkey mind was a flailing untrained simian, desperately beating the water in an attempt to stay afloat. I wanted to teach my mind to roll over, extend the limbs in relaxation, and to simply float atop the sea regardless of the waves churning below.

Since I had no prior experience in monkey-training, I enrolled in a 28 day meditation challenge that came complete with supporting materials. Somehow, I thought that my monkey would be intimidated into submission by the weight of the books and CDs alone. In the beginning, I distracted my monkey mind with ritual: candles, incense, music, and pillows placed just so. Only then would I recline and begin to unite with my breath.

Days passed with consistent meditation. And then weeks. Slowly, I began to forget to light the candles or pre-charge my iPod. I noticed it didn't matter; my monkey was beginning to tame. He still can't quite float, but at least he is not at risk for drowning anymore.

I found wisdom in the teachings of yoga and meditation. In both you are taught to find your edge, accept your edge, explore your edge (not to pretend it is not there and continue forward nonetheless, as I was wont to do). Pain is not something to be denied, but rather it should be acknowledged and investigated. I learned to recognize my bounds and slowly, softly shift them. I became more comfortable just being with the pain, softening my attitude towards it. The process of healing from the trauma made me softer, and that in turn made me stronger and more whole.

Strength found its balance in softness. The two together are so much more powerful than each alone. Try as I might, I still can't walk through furniture, though.

Lessons From the End of a Marriage

Lesson Seventeen

The end of a marriage does not mean the end of love.

1999

Timothy's mom wrote the following on our guest registry at our wedding reception:

> *"Timothy, I remember the day you said you would marry Lisa. You were 16. I was thrilled then and, if possible, I am even more so now."*

When I look back at those pictures from the wedding and all those snapshots of Timothy and I falling in love, it feels like the phantom pain of an amputated limb. He is so familiar. I look at the images and I remember his smell, the feeling of his breath on the top of my head, and the sound of his voice. He is so familiar, yet he is gone forever, the pictures merely an apparition. The love that is so apparent in the photos is also gone; the tender moments captured on film a relic of the past are as dead as the marriage they spawned.

I can't expect to have again what I had with Timothy. It was an illusion no more real than those pictures. I want reality and all that comes with it. He was only a "perfect" husband because it was all a lie. The reality will be messier, yet sweeter.

Winter 2010-2011

When I first started dating again, I was guarded. I was ready to date rather quickly, but not quite ready to fully trust or to completely open up to another. I viewed dating as a fun pastime, an opportunity to do things, get to meet new people, and learn more about myself. I had no expectations, no goals, and no objectives. I kept myself at a safe distance by telling my story early (just imagine hearing about a bigamist soon-to-be-ex-husband on a first date!) and informing my date that I was planning on moving to Seattle in a few months. I let myself be attracted, but I kept my heart in reserve, hiding my vulnerabilities and projecting an aura of self-sufficiency. I didn't make it easy to get to know me and I was happy that way.

That all changed with the receipt of a single e-mail with no text, only a picture of a dog.

Now, this wasn't just any dog. This was a six-month-old blue brindle pit bull puppy with a small body peeking out behind an enormous head. He had soft gray eyes with a mischievous glint. He had been christened "Tiger" in deference to the stripes that crossed his back. I had to meet this guy.

I had gone out with his owner, Brock, a couple times, but had not seen him in several weeks. I even (foolishly!) turned my head when he tried to kiss me after our second date. Brock sent the e-mail of his newly rescued dog to entice me to agree to another date. It worked. I'm a sucker for a cute puppy.

As Brock and I began spending more time together, I grew worried that my ability to trust had been thoroughly and inexorably damaged by my divorce. I had the utmost trust in my ex-husband. Even though we were very young when we began dating, I did not give up my trust easily; he earned it over years of proving himself reliable, dependable, and honest. Each time he followed through or stepped up, another deposit was made into the trust fund. I was hyper-vigilant about the fund in its early stages, carefully monitoring each deposit and looking for unexpected withdrawals. As time passed and the minimum account balance was ancient history, I began to relax.

And then, the unthinkable happened. The trust fund was emptied fully in one violent sweep as I learned of his years of lies and deceptions. It made me question the veracity of the 16 years of deposits. Were they forgeries? Fraud? Or, were they real enough and simply there for the taking?

I felt violated. Raped. Robbed. I trusted him to protect me from others and it turns out I needed protection from him.

It was an inside job.

I was left without a husband, but even more concerning, I was left with a damaged trust safe. Its integrity damaged by the robbery. It was no longer able to contain any deposits of trust. And I was afraid that it could not be repaired.

I began to work to repair the damage, patch the holes. I explored, finding and patching the weak areas. I tested its integrity by tentatively placing trust in others, yet ensuring that, if they were to fail to follow through, I would not be too badly compromised.

Time passed. The trust fund slipped from the forefront of my mind. I suppose I began to trust that it could contain wealth again, if it were to come my way.

Trust came through Tiger. He held nothing in reserve when we met. He greeted me as though I was his long lost buddy. He didn't care what baggage I brought or that I was still learning to have faith in others. He fully accepted me as I was at that moment. I didn't have to protect myself or worry about getting hurt. I didn't have to consider if he was truthful or hiding ulterior motives. I could trust him in a way that I couldn't trust anyone else.

Tiger was an ambassador of trust. Though I was not yet able to trust directly, he served as a bridge until I was able to open my heart yet again.

Tiger was not only a conduit of assurance, he was also a manifestation of Brock. We had taken to watching episodes of *The Dog Whisperer* with Cesar Milan. One of Cesar's favorite lines is, "I rehabilitate dogs; I train people." I can't say that I'm well-trained even after watching several seasons, but I certainly learned that the dog simply reflects the owner. If you see an anxious, unbalanced dog, it is a sign of the mental state of its owner.

I reflected back on the three dogs I had in my marriage. Max, the eldest was a Type A dog, in your face and seldom relaxed. She spent a lot of time with me. My driven nature was reflected in her. The middle dog, Porter, was primarily Timothy's. He was fearful-aggressive, letting anxiety build until he would snap. Not unlike what my husband ended up doing. Glottis, the last dog, was the most submissive. She came into the household after the lies and deceptions began. She spent much of her puppyhood with my husband as he worked at home at the time, but she still bonded more with me. She was an empathic dog and, in hindsight, she became despondent in those last several months. I may have ignored the warning signs being sounded by my sympathetic nervous system, but she did not. I cannot say that any of the dogs were truly balanced, nor were their owners.

Tiger, in contrast, was a balanced dog from the moment I met him. By watching him, I learned about Brock. People may be able to hide their true selves, but dogs cannot help but be honest. I saw a dog that was confident yet humble, not prone to anxiety or excess fear, and loved to exercise and chase tennis balls. Sure enough, these traits carried over from Brock.

In watching Brock and Tiger together, I learned to let go of some of my anxiety. I learned to trust and not hold the leash so tightly. I learned to laugh at the antics rather than worry about the result. I learned to observe without prior judgment.

Cesar's methodology worked in reverse in my case; a balanced dog helped me to find balance. And love.

Love is different the second time around. It has an entirely different texture than before. I will never again be the young girl in the pictures who had never experienced the pain of a broken heart. I am now bilingual; I speak the languages of love and loss, the two tongues enriching each other. I appreciate love so much more now that I have lived through its demise.

I listen more, yet I place less importance on words. Rather, I have learned to read the emotion behind the sentences and the actions after the promises. I am at once more independent, taking responsibility for my own happiness, and more willing to accept help and advice. I am mastering the art of managing my own anxiety without relying on Timothy's embraces to sooth me. Brock and I are together each day because we choose to be together each day.

Spring 2011

By that spring, I had been running for almost four years. From the beginning, I opted for traditional running shoes with layers of padding and rigid structures intended to support the feet and prevent injury. I believed the advertising: the more protection, the better. Perhaps because of a certain "devil may care" attitude from the divorce or simply out of a desire to try something new, I opted to replace my traditional running shoes with a pair of Vibrams, five-fingered minimalist running shoes that provide only the thinnest sliver of rubber and fabric between your feet and the elements. As I took my new shoes out for their inaugural runs, I realized they had as much to teach me about relationships as they did about running.

In regular running shoes, the thick outer sole prevents any contact between your foot and the ground; you are barely even aware of the different environments underfoot. In Vibrams, the thick sole allows you to discern the difference between soil and sand, asphalt and rock. It makes for a more fulfilling run as you connect with the earth underfoot. Likewise, allowing yourself to feel in a relationship makes the experience richer and more vibrant. Being aware of what is around you, tuning in to yourself and your partner, exposing the soul. It is scary to be vulnerable, both in foot and in feelings, but the rewards are worth the temporary discomfort.

I realized that the shields in the form of rigid outer bodies or internal walls are simply an illusion; they do not protect you from pain and injury. I learned that it is important to go slowly at the beginning, to allow the mind and body to adapt in stages to avoid becoming overwhelmed. As my running improved, I saw the importance of flexibility and adaptability and I carried those same skills home with me.

As I shed the weight and unyielding form of my old shoes that spring, I also learned how to be present in each step of my relationship and not shy away from the rocks underfoot. Lessons are everywhere when we are ready to listen.

Strangely enough, touring the end of a relationship has made it less scary to be committed. My fear of the unknown life without my husband has been replaced with the knowledge that I can undertake life's journey alone. I've ventured to that edge and survived. The end of a marriage does not have to mean the end of love, but maybe it does signal that it is time to buy new shoes.

Lessons From the End of a Marriage

Lesson Eighteen

Happiness is not a destination; it is a frame of mind.

March 2011

Late that previous fall, I received an e-mail from Brock.

"Wanna do this together?" was written above a link to Tough Mudder.

Intrigued, I clicked the link to see what he was suggesting. Tough Mudder, then still in its infancy, is a 10 to 12 mile obstacle run through challenging off-road trails. I had run Tough Mudder's baby cousin, the Warrior Dash, the year before and had a blast, but I could tell this was at a whole new level. With building excitement and trepidation, I clicked on the link that described the course.

As I looked through the descriptions of the obstacles: ice water swims and tunnel crawls, electric wires, and impossibly steep and muddy inclines, I realized this event was aptly named. This was no fun run. This was hours of muddy hell designed by ex-special forces. This would be a brutal challenge.

I said yes.

I was taming the inner voice that always told me I couldn't. I decided to tackle this challenge to prove to my inner negater that I damn well could.

We awoke to temperatures in the high 30s on the morning of the event. We would be lucky if the mercury rose to 50 by the finish of our run. We dressed lightly in technical fabrics, choosing bare wet skin over water-drenched clothing in the cold air. Once we arrived at the site, a motocross track in its other life, we met with another couple that we had planned to run with. After experiencing traditional road races, one of my favorite aspects of Tough Mudder was that it emphasizes teamwork and camaraderie. Even though we were officially a group of four, we soon found that all two thousand participants were one vast team.

With a bunch of rowdy chants and grunts (no one ever said this was a tea party), we were off. After a short dash through the trees, we were quickly directed to swim across an ice-filled river. Twice. The confidence and boisterousness washed away in the frigid water, the Mudders on the far shore shivering echoes of those who entered the stream.

Brock looked at me, took my hand, and said, "You'll be fine. We'll do this together."

I guess he heard the whispers of the doubting voice in my head.

The river was followed by a mile or so of straight running. Now this, I could do. I relaxed into the experience and let the cold fall from the forefront of my thoughts as I enjoyed the feeling of my legs warming through rhythmic movement. My confidence was short lived, however, as we came upon a low wooden structure filled with smoke. I could feel my throat closing and my lungs seizing even though the obstacle was still a hundred yards away.

"I can't. I'll have an asthma attack," looking over at Brock with fear building in my eyes. Memories of prior attacks, the gripping in the chest and the feeling of trying to suck air in through a straw, filled my head.

"Try. Just try. I'll stay with you," his hand on my back providing comfort while gently propelling me forward.

I agreed, aware at some level that my fear of the smoke's effects was much more powerful than the smoke itself. Tentatively, I lifted the black plastic sheet that held the smoke inside, and peered into the darkness. I could just make out the shifting forms of other Mudders as they crawled on their bellies under the low beams. I got down to my knees, took one last deep breath of unsullied air, and began to wriggle through the mud that covered the ground beneath the smoke. I was so focused on the destination, the slight glint of sunlight under the tarp in front of me, that I never thought about breathing. When I reached the end, and burst through the hanging plastic into the clear air, I suddenly realized I had not experienced any difficulty in breathing after I let go of the panic.

When I said I *couldn't* breathe in the smoke, I actually meant I *wouldn't* breathe in the smoke. That single shift of a letter belying the importance in the shift in meaning. Unlike the certainty of "I can't," I can choose what I will or will not do.

My nemesis behind me, we continued our journey through the muddy madness. Twenty foot walls that would be unscalable alone were traversed with the helping hands of dozens of Mudders. We crossed slanted and slicked monkey bars, gripping tightly to avoid the water below. We ran up hills until we had to walk or even crawl. We ran through fire only to plunge back into biting water. As we grew tired, we all had moments of doubt, but we were able to bury the doubt in the miles of mud we left behind. Finally, with a shocking finale, we ran under the live wires and into the welcoming arms of the volunteers who held out food, water, and warming blankets.

I became a Tough Mudder to silence my inner apprehension, to prove to myself that I can. I realized how often, "I can't" is fear's way of saying, "I won't."

I always said that I couldn't live without Timothy. By facing down those other challenges, and coming through them stronger and more confident, I learned that I could. And I would.

I chose to frame the period of time around my divorce as a series of lessons; it helped to create purpose out of tragedy and encouraged me to learn from the past while moving towards the future. It also reminds me that I am never done; there is always more to learn. I am encouraged in this view by Brock, who sees himself as a perpetual student, always willing and eager to learn something new, even in an area where he is considered an expert.

Last year, we were out at dinner with a group of friends. One of our friend's eight-year-old son opened the conversation with my boyfriend, a martial arts instructor.

"Do you have a black belt?" the boy asked eagerly.

"I do," came the reply.

"Actually, he has several," interjected the boy's dad.

"Wow! Does that mean you know everything?"

"Actually, a black belt means that you are ready to begin learning."

I loved that response. It serves as a reminder to me to always be open to learning more, especially in those areas where one already has knowledge. I am currently learning that a messy kitchen does not indicate a chaotic life; it just means that people actually live in my house. I am still working on going downhill and accepting that it is okay to slow down sometimes. I try to practice gratitude every day. Especially when the kitchen is messy.

Life isn't like the movies; not every story wraps up neatly, presented in a gift bag with a matching bow. I wish I could say that Timothy has served his time in prison, has made amends to those he wronged, and is now living a virtuous life after facing down the hard truths of karma. I want to tell you about how Amanda escaped his grasp and is now traveling the world with her own Brock (not the same one; however, we've already been there). I would love to inform you that Timothy's parents are well and have established a relationship with their son that they never had before. I wish I could tell you those stories, but I cannot. I do not know how their stories have unfolded or where life has seen fit to take them. I can only hope that they are receptive to their own lessons.

As for me, I am happy, but I no longer believe in "ever after" as a destination. Rather, happiness is something that I strive for every day and in every moment. I work to approach my past with humility and the future with curiosity. I have embraced the lessons that I have learned and identified many that I still need to work on.

I still have moments of heartache when my husband's face flashes before my eyes and I feel his arms around me once again. There are times when I feel the bottomless pit of confusion and sorrow that engulfed me with a text. The anger occasionally sparks, catching me off guard with its ferocity and raw power. But mostly, I look back with a mixture of sadness and gratitude; mourning what was lost but thankful for what has been gained.

I have found a balance in my life that was missing before. I have learned to allow softness to permeate where before there was only steel. I am working on calming my mind and finding acceptance in place of resistance. My life no longer jumps over the pauses in my to-do list like a skipping record; I now celebrate the in-betweens. I am learning to not let fear be my chauffeur and to take chances where I would have stopped short before. I am better about accepting what is rather then trying to force my will on everything. I have learned to find my voice and I am using it to help others navigate their own journeys through divorce and into wellness. I am learning from the stories of others and becoming aware of how similar the human experience is beneath the varied surfaces.

My autopilot is now permanently disabled; I am flying through life with eyes wide open and hopefully with karma at my back.

Conclusion

I'm often asked if I've ever heard from him. I never have, and I expect I never will. This is the message I would like to think he has composed, even if it remains forever unsent.

Lisa,

First, I want to say how sorry I am. I never wanted this to happen to you. To us. My intent was never to hurt you. I started lying to protect you from some stupid decisions I made. I thought I could fix it, but it just got more out of control. I think that's when the depression started. I know it's when I started drinking too much. It got to the point where I didn't know what was real and what was fabricated. I was lost and, unfortunately, I took you along on my dark ride.

Our relationship was real. I'm sure you've wondered. It was very real; my love for you was real. I told you once when we were teenagers that you saved me. I meant it, but I guess I was too far gone to be completely saved.

I hope that you're happy and that you have been able to move on. I hope that you have found someone else who is honest with you. You deserve it.

I'm still working on my problems. I'm seeing someone to help with the lying and the drinking. It's hard, but I'm making progress. I'm learning to take responsibility for what I've done and how I feel.

I treasure the memories of our time together and I hope that you are able to look back and smile too.

Sometimes in my dreams, the clown still walks at midnight and we still have all our days ahead of us.

Timothy

This would be my final message to him.

Timothy,

How did it ever come to this? I still have such a difficult time reconciling what happened to the man I loved. I wish you would have gotten help years ago. I would have joined the fight with you. Instead, I've been forced to fight against you. I wish I would have noticed how far you had strayed. I wish I had managed my anxiety better. I wish we could have worked together on our marriage the way we worked together on everything else. The results have been so tragic.

None of that matters now. We're here. Wishes won't change that.

You have brought me the greatest joys and the greatest sorrows in life, but I am not dependent upon you for either. I am responsible for my own happiness in life; I choose to make my life meaningful and joyful, regardless of the hell you dragged me through. I refuse to be defined by or limited by your choices; I am only limited by myself. July was my rebirth. But it was a terrible delivery.

I really hope that, wherever you are, you're okay. I hope that you are making choices that do not harm you or anyone else around you. I hope that you are taking responsibility for the harm you've done. I hope that you are shedding whatever demons overshadowed you and that your true self is able to see the sun again.

I still have such fond memories of our time together. I think about so many moments and smile. And sometimes cry. I loved you, utterly and completely. Perhaps I loved you too much for I failed to see you as a fallible man and, as such, I didn't recognize your suffering in time to help save you. For that, I am truly sorry.

Your actions shocked and hurt me more than you can probably imagine. I've changed. Possibly so much that you wouldn't even know me now. Your choices pruned me back to the core, but I have been able to grow new branches from the wounds. Life is beautiful. I hope that you have been able to find beauty in your life and that you can help bring it to others.

I often think of belt sanders on tile, and I smile alone.

Lisa

July 2012

Lessons From the End of a Marriage

Acknowledgments

I (much less the book) would not be here without the support of so many people. I could not have done this alone.

Cathy Arends – Thank you for always being my support and sounding board, providing feedback and encouragement. It's been a wild ride, but we have made it through.

Tommy Arends – I don't know what I would have done if you were not there those first few days. Thank you for picking me up off the floor and staying with me for the long haul.

Sarah, Curtis, and Kayla – Thank you for providing me with my "Ronald McDonald House for the recently separated." Your generosity and friendship is amazing.

Ben – Thank you for being more than just an officer. You brought sanity and hope into the darkest days.

Christian – Thank you for always being a listening ear and a welcoming shoulder on those days and nights I didn't think I could make it.

Tiger – Thank you for teaching me how to trust again. And, yes, you can have a cookie.

Brock – I feel so lucky that you came into my life. I love our Tamley. Thank you for showing me that I can love again.

Thank you to all my family who provided money, humor, and support from across the country. I never felt alone with balm squad at my side.

Thank you to all my friends in Atlanta who found homes for my dogs, covered my classroom when I needed to call the lawyers, fed me when I wouldn't eat on my own, and made sure that I had opportunities to be social.
Thank you to those who took care of my dogs when I wasn't able. You brought me peace.

Thank you to those who helped me craft my story by tirelessly giving me feedback and suggestions.

Thank you to all of the followers on my blog, Facebook, and Twitter who have given me encouragement on the "down days," celebrated each victory with me, and been willing to share their own stories.

Thank you to all of those that I came across in my journey who offered a hug, a smile, or an encouraging word. You have no idea how much each of you meant to me.

You all are my heroes.

About the Author

Lisa Arends, BS, MEd

Certified Nutrition and Wellness Consultant and Personal Trainer

Lisa Arends works as a math teacher and a wellness coach. After using her own sudden divorce three years ago as a catalyst for positive change, she now helps people navigate their own divorces. She loves to lift heavy weights and run long distances, and she is still learning how to meditate.

You can find more of Lisa's lessons as well as the lessons of others (and cute pictures of Tiger!) on Lisa's blog at **http://lessonsfromtheendofamarriage.com**.

You can also find Lisa on Facebook (**Lessons From the End of a Marriage**) and Twitter (**@stilllearning2b**).

You're good, but you can be better.
http://actionpotentialwellness.com

Made in the USA
Lexington, KY
09 October 2012